START
LIVING
EVERY DAY
OF
YOUR LIFE

START LIVING EVERY DAY OF YOUR LIFE

How to use the Science of Mind

MARGARET R. STORTZ

Science of Mind Publications
Los Angeles, California

THIRD PRINTING - JUNE 1988
Copyright © 1981 by Science of Mind Publications

Published by Science of Mind Publications
3251 West Sixth Street—P.O. Box 75127
Los Angeles, California 90075

Printed in the United States of America

ISBN 0-911336-87-7

Cover design: Robert R. Tompkins

CONTENTS

INTRODUCTION

THIS WONDERFUL book was written to be *used* . . . by you or by anyone else who desires a happier, more prosperous, more loving life. It is based on the simple idea that the universe is basically harmonious, and that if we live in accordance with this fundamental universal harmony, we will be free, joyous, and creative people.

But how do we live "in accordance with universal harmony"?

The American philosopher Ernest Holmes (1887–1960) taught that we can do so by first adjusting our *minds* in the direction of harmony. We must train our thoughts, reshaping our mental patterns so they coincide with the ways we want to be. Because this reshaping produces results through the operation of natural principles, Dr. Holmes recognized that his method was truly scientific . . . a *science of mind!*

He presented these ideas in his classic book, *The Science of Mind* (Dodd, Mead & Co., 1938), which has gone through forty-one printings and inspired millions of people worldwide. *Science of Mind* Magazine also carries this message of optimism and well-being to additional tens of thousands on a monthly basis.

The book you are holding in your hands is a simple, down-to-earth presentation of Ernest Holmes' basic ideas, written by someone who has used and taught these ideas professionally for many years. As a Science of Mind Practitioner, Margaret Stortz has provided spiritual aid to countless people, and through her contributions to *Science of Mind* Magazine, she has inspired thousands of others throughout the world.

Start Living Every Day of Your Life is compiled from Mrs. Stortz' writings in *Science of Mind* Magazine over a period of twelve years. Divided into five major categories, it deals specifically with matters of love, health, money, personal expression, and the joys of being alive. Each commentary is followed by a segment of text in boldface type, which is intended to be read aloud, perhaps several times, with deep feeling and sincere intention. This is what begins the process of reshaping your mental patterns, and you should repeat it on a daily basis until you begin to feel the truth of what the material says. You will also note quotations from the Bible, which is a spiritual resource for many people in the Western world, and from *The Science of Mind,* by Ernest Holmes. These references, which support the ideas in the main text, may prove helpful.

A great adventure awaits you as you consciously align yourself with the harmony of the universe. Peace, prosperity, and love are yours to have. This book can be the beginning point for the most exciting journey you will ever undertake— your journey of self-discovery and enlightenment as you *start living every day of your life!*

—*Science of Mind Publications*

I

To Your Health

I CANNOT tell you how to live, but I can tell you this: If you live a stressful, anxious life, sooner or later you will get sick. I know this because I have seen too many negative attitudes turn into too many painful illnesses in too many bodies. I have also seen what good, determined use of positive attitudes and ideas can do toward bringing a person back to a healthy state.

Good health begins in the mind, and it starts with the formation of attitudes that bring life and vigor to the body. Your body will be happy to oblige you if you give it something it can use to promote its own well-being.

The ideas on the following pages are designed to help you do something about the state of your health. If it is already good, these readings will help keep you in a state of uninterrupted good health. If you would like to feel better, these readings will help you to achieve a glowing state of health that you may have forgotten all about.

I believe you were meant to be healthy. I believe you were meant to enjoy life. And I believe you can do both of these things if you take charge of your own mind now!

Here's to your Health!

1

I AM THE PICTURE OF HEALTH

HOW MANY of us realize that in back of the image we see whenever we look at ourselves in a mirror is a Divine image? The face looking back at us pictures infinite Life as It is channeled into our personal selves. Sometimes, however, that picture gets out of focus when the thought of illness obscures the Divine perfection. Very subtly, our bodies manifest the illness that ideas of sickness, fear, and anxiety produce. Human nature tends to dwell on the symptoms of disease rather than on the image of wholeness that is God's nature. But while illness may be a momentary fact, it cannot be an eternal truth about any of us.

God is never sick, never in pain, never uncomfortable. As manifestations of God, we need not embody disease and suffering. Our heritage is one of perfect well-being. As long as we center our attention on the infinite Self that is always circulating wholesome Life-energy through us, we begin to respect our bodies; we acquire healthier living habits, and more consistently assume sound mental patterns that externalize as physical health. And the mirrored picture we see radiates the spirited vitality that is ours.

I *know* that God has created me a whole, healthy being. From head to toe, I radiate strength and energy. Disease has no place in me, and I carefully guard my thoughts to prevent any false ideas from gaining a foothold in my consciousness. I see myself as the perfect picture of life, unfettered by my former thoughts of ill-health. I am conscious of a perfect functioning in every part of my body, down to the tiniest cell. I bless my body, and I know that it always acts in accordance with Divine intent.

Beloved, I wish above all things that thou mayest prosper and be in health, even as thy soul prospereth. —III John 2

. . . LET US REMEMBER THAT BACK OF THE MAN WHICH WE SEE IS THE DIVINE IMAGE. —*The Science of Mind*, page 196

THE FIFTH FREEDOM

GOOD HEALTH is a fact of our divinity. Since God gives alike to each, it simply is not true that some people must spend their physical lives in a peevish and unhealthy rut, apparent victims of a frail physical condition. Any inherited tendency is simply that, a *tendency*, and if it's unhealthy, it can be changed. More than one famous athlete began life as a sickly child, only to overcome the physical handicap and even surpass his healthier companions.

The only "weather" to which our bodies are subject is our inner state of mind, our "inner plane" weather. And our bodies are weather vanes; they show to all the world whether we have raging storms inwardly or well-balanced flows of growth and development.

Our physical health is also one of the best and most immediate indicators of spiritual growth. Since all mental states will actualize in our outer world eventually, we will see our spiritual vigor effectively demonstrated in bodies that quicken in liveliness and energy. Good health should be the rule, not the exception in our lives.

I thank God for my beautiful, healthy body! Because I am part of the perfect creative Power which endows life with the necessary zest and energy for expression, I accept nothing less than happy, wholesome days of effective living. In mind and body, I live a balanced life, nourishing my consciousness with spiritual truths while I wisely care for my physical body and its special needs. God expresses through me now as unobstructed, radiant wholeness!

The light of the body is the eye: if therefore thine eye be single, thy whole body shall be full of light. —Matthew 6:22

WE ARE LIMITED, NOT BY PRINCIPLE, BUT BY OUR OWN INABILITY TO SEE PERFECTION. —*The Science of Mind*, page 197

THE KEY TO GOOD HEALTH

E RNEST HOLMES says that our general mental tendency reflects itself in our bodies. Therefore, if our thought patterns are optimistic, enthusiastic, and expectant of good, the state of our health should be good. But if we are critical, pessimistic, and unable to look for the good in life, our bodies become super-sensitive to everything toxic in our surroundings. Many physicians are inclined to agree that certain deep, negative emotions such as hate, grief, and resentment are apt to bring on some diseases.

Let me add to this list of early warning signals: a poor self-image. For example, some people can spend years waiting for death to arrive simply because they feel it is not worthwhile to keep on living. However, sickness and death do not solve any problems . . . they simply put off what we must learn eventually to handle. We might as well acknowledge the fact that our thoughts about ourselves and others affect the quality of our lives, and it is much better *now* to set about weaving the most healthful and inspired thought patterns we can.

The Universal Life and I are one—one in spiritual inspiration, one in matured thought, one in physical action. I accept good spiritual thought patterns as the basis for healthy, harmonious living. I value my importance to life, and I cease to waste time and energy indulging in negativity. Today I begin to shape the fabric of my thoughts with the expectancy of good health, and I am grateful to God for help in this area.

For ye shall go out with joy, and be led forth with peace . . . .
—Isaiah 55:12

A NORMAL HEALTHY MIND REFLECTS ITSELF IN A HEALTHY BODY, AND CONVERSELY, AN ABNORMAL MENTAL STATE EXPRESSES ITS CORRESPONDING CONDITION IN SOME PHYSICAL CONDITION.
—*The Science of Mind,* page 144

GOD IS PERFECT HEALTH

WE ARE MADE in accordance with a spiritual pattern of perfection and our bodies are the exact reflections of this pattern. But in our daily living this does not always appear to be the case. How often do we see sick bodies, which certainly cannot be the reflection of a Divine wholeness? What has happened to disrupt that which should be a completely healthy joining of body and Spirit? *Our mentalities are the variable factor.* Because the gift of choice has been bestowed upon us, we often choose unwisely and obstruct the flow of perfect Spirit through an otherwise nonresistant body.

Ideally, Spirit, mind, and body should work in perfect coordination. Spirit is the initiating factor, mind the correct interpreter, and body the undemanding example. In the complete, undisturbed unity of these three levels of life lies our good health. Thus, along with intelligent care of the body, we need to keep our minds alert and receptive to Spirit, which is perfection and needs no tampering with by us. When we are receptive to Spirit, sickness, which is unnatural, shall disappear from our experience and good health return in all its fullness.

The Universal Life and I are one—one in spiritual inspiration, one in matured thought, one in physical action. I am the whole, healthy creation of God. I accept the teaching of Spirit within me and keep my mind turned to Its healthful activities. My body is the resilient reflection of sound thinking. My choices are wise; Spirit in me is not deterred from Its work, and I am grateful for the demonstration of good health in my life.

. . . I am the Lord that healeth thee. —Exodus 15:26

THE PERFECT MAN IS THE ONLY MAN GOD KNOWS!
—*The Science of Mind,* page 338

PRAYER IS THE BEST MEDICINE

FROM THE movie *Elmer Gantry,* one line stands out that we might all take to heart. In the film the preacher says: "Prayin's the cheapest first-rate medicine I know!"

When the body is in pain, a physician will often prescribe medicine to relieve the experience of pain. But in some instances we may be moved to realize where it first began—in our minds and hearts. Then we must turn in prayer to the Source of our healing, and that doesn't cost a single cent!

Through prayer, we can communicate actively with God. In times of prayer we set aside our ordinary preoccupation with mundane appearances and turn our attention to the true center of our universe. Prayer is our refuge and refreshment, and when we pray, it opens the channel through which we receive God's "medicine" for use in every circumstance. Unlike the usual prescription which must be used sparingly, we may turn to God in prayer constantly, for our relief is never withheld from us. We must simply trust and accept it.

With a prayer always on my lips, I turn within to God throughout the day. There is no challenge to which I am not equal nor any task I cannot handle, for I rely, not on my own devices, but on the energies and directives of the inner Presence. I am healed in mind, body, and experience. I gratefully embody the consciousness of wholeness which comes through my prayerful attitude and I accept what has already been showered on me by God.

And all things, whatsoever ye shall ask in prayer, believing, ye shall receive. —Matthew 21:22

THROUGH PRAYER WE RECOGNIZE A SPIRITUAL LAW, THAT HAS ALWAYS EXISTED, AND PUT OURSELVES IN ALIGNMENT WITH IT.
—*The Science of Mind,* page 152

THE HEALING ATMOSPHERE

AMONG THOSE who work in the spiritual fields, there is a great desire to create and maintain a healing awareness, a certain kind of "atmosphere." We remember the story about the woman who simply touched the hem of Jesus' garment and was made whole, so great was the wholeness that emanated from him.

We may not yet have attained such an exalted degree of spiritual "emission," but we can know we are practicing spiritual Truth properly when people come to us and say, "I feel so good just being around you!" They sense what we have been cultivating, whether it is experienced as a great degree of God-Love or simply a feeling of deep peace. If we are consistent in our spiritual work, eventually it is bound to become incorporated into our being and to be emitted as a wonderful, positive feeling.

God is the Sublime Essence of Life, and because I am One with God, Life in Its fullness is mine. I am a vessel accepting Divine fulfillment, and I pour forth the contents of love, peace, and good thoughts upon all I meet. I am never emptied of good, and all those around me are touched by my atmosphere in a positive way. My inner order, reflected in my subconscious attitudes, makes me a force for good, right where I am.

Let your light so shine before men, that they may see your good works, and glorify your Father which is in heaven. —Matthew 5:16

BY GIVING OUR COMPLETE ATTENTION TO ANY ONE IDEA WE AUTOMATICALLY EMBODY IT. —*The Science of Mind,* page 411

'TIS THE SEASON TO BE HEALTHY

W E ARE meant to enjoy good health, but we forever see the picture of ill health before us, either in ourselves or in others. So we may help ourselves by looking at the roots from which our health springs.

Let's consider these three basic tenets: (1) *We are intended to be healthy.* If we are the products of a perfect Creator, which can only give perfectly, then something is wrong on the receiving end of things when we find ourselves unhealthy. There are mental matters that need tending. (2) *The body is the indicator of our health, not the initiator of it.* The body is Spirit in Its densest form, the last place where our mental marvels (or disasters) shall be mirrored. The body does not decide to be healthy or sick. We, by our thought-trends, sway it one way or the other. (3) *Thought-trends are cumulative.* We will never begin a new day free from the vestiges of yesterday's thought unless we deliberately make the attempt to do so. Therefore, our thought-trends must be as uplifting, enthusiastic, and inspiring as we can make them if we are to enjoy consistent good health.

There is one perfect Whole, one Spiritual Life, complete and limitless. I am one with this Life of Wholeness, an unrestricted agent through which the Divine Presence flows. I think healthy thoughts. I concentrate on healthy activities. Therefore, my body is outpicturing good health. I am grateful to God for the gifts of strength, vigor, and enthusiasm, and I protect them with right thoughts.

. . . and if the root be holy, so are the branches.   —Romans 11:16

THE PERFECT MAN IS THE ONLY MAN GOD KNOWS!
                                        —*The Science of Mind*, page 338

YOU'RE AS YOUNG AS YOU WANT TO BE

FEW OF US us would like to remain children forever, but we would often like to feel young a lot longer than we do. We would like to enjoy a perpetual springtime of living and avoid the wintry chill that may come in later years.

There are some people who manage this quite delightfully. I think of a charming friend of mine, nearly 80, who once told me, "Every time I look into a mirror, I'm always surprised to see that old face looking out at me!" Young in spirit, she remains vital and interesting, even though her body is aging.

We should remember that our bodies need not affect our youthful spirit. Our true age is determined by us mentally, for we shall remain as young and flexible as we choose to think. God, the Essence of our life, is ageless. We, therefore, are as timeless as the Universe itself.

When we are constantly revitalized by contact with the vibrant Spirit of Life, we are bound to maintain an ebullient freshness. Our minds will stay young forever, and our bodies, always subject to the direction of our mental states, will age in unfoldment, rather than infirmity.

I am one with the timeless Essence of Life. I appreciate this Life and let It flow through my thoughts and acts. I listen to Its nourishments and manifest Its youthful qualities. I listen to Its instructions. I am vital, youthful, and flexible. I accept new ideas.

. . . therefore glorify God in your body, and in your spirit, which are God's. —I Corinthians 6:20

SUCH AN UNDERSTANDING TEACHES US THAT THERE CAN NEVER COME A TIME WHEN WE SHALL STOP PROGRESSING; THAT AGE IS AN ILLUSION. . . . —*The Science of Mind,* page 180

RESISTANCE TO ILLNESS

MANY PEOPLE actually open the door to illness at certain seasons of the year. Armed with liniments and medicines, they go forth fully prepared for their first winter cold, or the hay fever season, or whatever malady they expect to have. We may know some of these people; or, unwittingly, we may be among them!

Much negative advertising is done through magazines and television. Consciously, we may not appear to be paying attention to these commercials. However, knowing the great susceptibility of the subconscious mind, can we be sure that it is not responding to this negativity? Therefore, we should mentally refuse to accept these undesirable possibilities when they come within the range of our sight or hearing.

Infinite Life has provided the pattern and necessary functions for our blossoming good health on a year-'round basis. There is no reason why we should expect to become ill simply because the season changes. Sickness in any form is not God-ordained. Only good health is intended for us, so let's accept it.

There is one Life, that Life is God, and that Life is my life now. This Life is forever whole, complete, and perfect. There is never any lessening of Its wholeness, and nothing can disturb the harmonious Life within me. So there is no reason why my health should vary with the seasons of the year. I discard such notions right now, and accept instead the blessing of constant good health. I am immune from the mental stress and negative suggestions that cause illness. Strength, vitality, and well-being are my Divine inheritance, and I gratefully accept radiant good health.

. . . According to your faith be it unto you.   —Matthew 9:29

IF THE BODY IS TO BE PERMANENTLY WELL, THE SOUL OR SUBJECTIVE LIFE MUST BE IN POISE, THE MIND PEACEFUL AND HAPPY. . . . WHEN THE SOUL IS POISED IN TRUE SPIRITUAL REALIZATION THE BODY WILL BE NORMAL AND HEALTHY.   —*The Science of Mind,* page 99

HERE'S TO YOUR HEALTH

THERE CAN be great value in asking questions of ourselves. Such questioning causes us to rethink ideas we had taken for granted, or it may bring to light hidden values we had forgotten.

Do we accept perfect health as our God-given heritage? Do we daily bless every cell in our bodies? Do we think of our bodies as the magnificent palaces which house our true Being? Do we give our bodies at least the same care that we give our most prized possessions? Do we watch the tendency our thoughts are taking, carefully screening out all negativity before it has a chance to "set"?

If we can answer "yes" to all these questions, our "health quotient" will be excellent. If there are doubts or negative answers, however, we can see the areas that need work in bringing us closer to a Divine standard of health. It is time to see ourselves as perfect creations of a Perfect Creator.

God *is perfect Life.* **This Life circulates through every atom of my body-temple. I accept with thanksgiving my perfect health as a continuing legacy from God.**

I now eliminate any doubts or questions about my worth, my competence, or my wholeness. I see my body and its care from a new, healthy perspective; and I respect the importance that this physical organism has in enabling me to express my life perfectly. I give thanks that I am radiantly healthy now!

A wicked messenger falleth into mischief: but a faithful ambassador is health. —Proverbs 13:17

MAN IS FUNDAMENTALLY PERFECT, THIS IS OUR WHOLE PREMISE—PERFECT GOD, PERFECT MAN, PERFECT BEING. . . .
—*The Science of Mind,* page 201

WE ARE MADE IN PERFECTION

THE RENOWNED psychiatrist Carl Jung presents the idea of God as being an *archetype*. He said that "the idea of an all-powerful divine being is present everywhere, if not consciously recognized, then unconsciously accepted. . . ." God, then, is the original Pattern from which all creation stems. If, as the Science of Mind philosophy holds, the Divine Pattern is perfect, we therefore must be made in Perfection.

What happens to us when we become ill? Surely our perfect molds have not become defective. No, hardly that! But, in the words of the New Testament writer, we "see through a glass darkly," and spiritual truths are obscured from our view by the cloudiness of our imperfect viewpoints. We do not always adhere to the spiritual patterns from which we were constructed and whenever a false idea comes strongly between us and the idea of Perfection, our bodies tend to become ill.

Through prayer and meditation, therefore, we should keep our gaze concentrated upon the perfect qualities of God, maintaining our minds and bodies in right alignment with Divine nature.

God is my Creator. His Life, Love, and Intelligence animate my body. I accept my body as the properly functioning physical effect of Divine ideas, and I allow no false impression to upset its operation. I attune my thoughts to God's Presence, and am receptive only to those ideas which are good and purposeful. I am always healthy, as I live according to God's will.

. . . *According to your faith be it unto you.*　　　　　—Matthew 9:29

IN OUR IGNORANCE OF THE TRUTH, WE HAVE MISUSED THE HIGHEST POWER WE POSSESS.　　　　　—*The Science of Mind,* page 36

GOOD HEALTH IS OUR HERITAGE

WE SHOULD realize that we are meant to be healthy. Only when we create a belief in inherited tendencies, or in the inevitability of disease, or in destructive patterns of mind, do things begin to go wrong. Our bodies are miracles of creation which constantly renew and restore themselves through subtle biological and chemical activities beyond our comprehension. Even the most sophisticated scientist watches in awe. So, since we can appreciate the amazing Intelligence at work in our bodies, we must consciously determine not to disturb Its orderly activity through negative thinking.

We believe in a God who has given us His life; we know that Life is Perfect and that the potentiality of Its Perfection lies in each one of us. Therefore we must see ourselves as God sees us—as expressions of our own complete Self—with no barriers to limit this Self-expression. The Infinite placed the seed of Perfection in each person, and the flowering of that true nature should be permitted to occur without obstruction.

I am created with the essence of Perfect Being. I know and accept that Divine Intelligence controls every function of my body, and I cease to disturb or constrict it. Perfect health is my Divine heritage—nothing less—and I accept it now. The one Life—perfect, whole, and complete—is my life today. I live in this consciousness, keeping my thoughts aligned with ideas of health.

Not that we are sufficient of ourselves to think any thing as of ourselves; but our sufficiency is of God. . . . —II Corinthians 3:5

THE SPIRITUAL MAN IS CONTINUOUSLY REMOLDING AND REMAKING THE MATERIAL, OR PHYSICAL MAN. —*The Science of Mind*, page 317

YOU CAN BE HEALTHY

SOME PEOPLE seem to treat their health as if it were determined by the toss of a coin. Heads, you get good health; tails, you don't! They apparently feel, if their health is bad, that they are one of those poor, frail creatures destined to live in a weakened condition.

But does it seem reasonable that God, the Giver of all Good, would decide that some shall have health and some shall not? Not if we really live in a universe which is innately good and orderly!

The state of our health, therefore, is determined by *us*, by ourselves, and nothing other than our thoughts and attitudes stands in the way of God's perfect gift of well-being. We can choose to accept these gifts, or we can decide not to. The determination is made by us . . . not by a roll of some cosmic dice. Why, then, do problems of ill-health ordinarily seem to come upon us without our having chosen them? Because we haven't yet seen the connection between our attitudes and what those attitudes cause. The mind-body connection is real, and if we don't take charge of our thoughts and feelings, we shall find that our bodies may soon reflect the idea that sickness is just as likely to happen as wellness.

God, the only Life there is, and I are joyously one. As God's creation, I am a desired, worthwhile expression of Life. No past mistakes I may have made, nor other people's opinions, can alter that fact. Therefore, the good things of life, including good health, are meant to be mine. I accept wholeness joyfully and I live the active life which attends good health. I am grateful, for I am healthy.

For as the Father hath life in himself; so hath he given to the Son to have life in himself. . . . —John 5:26

WE UNDERSTAND THAT HEALTH IS A MENTAL AS WELL AS A PHYSICAL STATE. —*The Science of Mind,* page 190

LOVE HEALS

MUCH HAS been said about the healing power of Love, for it is indeed a balm for every kind of wound. Love by its nature is non-agitating. It is innately soothing, peaceful, and harmonious; and when it is loosed in a circumstance, it, like a lotion or liniment, smoothly and easily fills in any area that is wanting.

By the tremendous power of Love, we may heal a body or we may heal a situation; for not only will it neutralize an imbalance in the body, but it will also bring peace and comfort to the sorrowing heart or the pressure-laden mind. Ernest Holmes said that "Love is the grandest healing and drawing power on earth," which suggests to us another aspect of the power of Love. Not only does it go forth into a situation, but it also attracts unto itself. If Love is permitted entry into an area where there is a lack of some sort, it will draw to itself whatever is needed for completion, whether that be friends, jobs, money, or anything else required. We are wise to be grateful for the many-splendored power of Love.

God, the only Life there is, and I are joyously one. Love fills my life, healing every rough area or symptom of sickness. Love brings peace and harmony to my every activity. The presence of Love in me draws to me everything and everyone necessary for my well-being. I am grateful for loving friends, satisfying endeavors, and robust health. As I am the instrument of Love, only good goes forth from me.

. . . their hearts might be comforted, being knit together in love. . . .
—Colossians 2:2

LOVE ALONE OVERCOMES ALL AND JUSTIFIES THE ETERNITY OF HER DOMINION. —*The Science of Mind,* page 460

SPIRIT KNOWS NO INCURABLE DISEASE

AS BELIEVERS in spiritual healing, we speak of the perfect wholeness of the Divine Spirit within us, and we do very well at revealing this innate wholeness when it comes to the healing of such things as cuts, colds, or broken limbs. But what happens to us when we are confronted with a disease that is labeled incurable, such as cancer or diabetes? We often falter, because we are caught up in established fears and opinions regarding such problems.

Ernest Holmes has told us that the Law of Mind does not know anything about big or little. He further states that "God cannot know anything which is contrary to the Divine Being." Therefore, if the healing Power heals anything, It can heal everything, and the differentiating factor must be present in ourselves! We experience greater fear in some circumstances than in others, and so we cut down the effectiveness of the God-Power within us. Let us remember Dr. Holmes' words of reassurance, and so dissipate our fears about any illness. Then no longer shall there be any such thing as a dread disease.

God, the only Life there is, and I are joyously one. I am the receptacle of God's perfect Life. I am not afraid of physical upsets, whether they be considered mild or severe. I know only that Spirit in me has the power to dissolve any unwanted condition. Therefore I am free from fear about my health. I think healthy thoughts, live a healthy life, and I am thankful that God in me can resolve any physical imbalance.

And we know that all things work together for good to them that love God, to them who are the called according to his purpose.
—Romans 8:28

GOD CANNOT KNOW ANYTHING WHICH IS CONTRADICTORY TO THE DIVINE BEING. —*The Science of Mind*, page 312

GOOD HEALTH IS OUR NATURAL ESTATE

A WISE TEACHER once said, "There is nothing to be healed, only Truth to be revealed." To the metaphysician this statement of deep understanding solemnizes his every prayer and perfectly characterizes his inward striving for Oneness with God. In Truth, in the pattern world of the Spirit, which precedes every physical manifestation, there can be no disturbance of any kind.

During his prayer work, the student of Truth seeks to know in the physical realm that which his God-self knows as actuality in Spirit. The greater his capacity for spiritual understanding, the better, quicker, and cleaner will be his demonstration.

Appearances of ill health, lack, or limitation of any kind have no power in themselves, only the power we give to them. When we cease to rivet our attention upon them, they tend to dissolve into the nothingness from which they came. When sometimes we are cast adrift upon the sea of unhappy effects which seem to swirl about us, it is time to head back to the shores of steadfast Truth, which will be our safe harbor.

There is only one Life, God's Life, and I am one with It. **I see myself as God sees me—perfect, radiantly healthy, and functioning in right accord with His Universe.**

I manifest in my physical life the wholeness that is spiritually mine. Therefore, I am an unconstricted channel of Truth, as through me Spirit dissolves anything unlike Itself. Thankfully I am free from limitation, for I no longer believe in it.

. . . I am the Lord that healeth thee. —Exodus 15:26

. . . HEALTH IS AN OMNIPRESENT REALITY, AND WHEN THE OBSTRUCTIONS THAT HINDER HEALING ARE REMOVED, IT WILL BE FOUND THAT HEALTH WAS THERE ALL THE TIME. —*The Science of Mind*, page 203

HEALTH AND HAPPINESS

THERE APPEARS to be a definite link between the state of our health and our ability to be happy. Unhealthy people are seldom happy, and happy people are healthy most of the time. This cannot be coincidental. Rather, it is another illustration of the fact which science is now beginning to confirm: There is an indissoluble link between habitual patterns of mind and the general state of one's health.

If we would have physical health, we must know that a healthy mind is its prerequisite, for all circumstances are formed in the mental realm before they are manifested in the physical world. It is well worth our time to turn daily to the Divine Presence for our dosage of calm confidence, inner peace, and constant guidance. We may begin each day knowing that we are receptacles of the Divine Good, carriers of productive ideas, and revealers of a Life of perfect intent. This will be our shield against the negative thoughts which can eventually cause sick bodies.

The one perfect Life of God is my life now.

As God cannot know anything imperfect, I basically cannot entertain imperfection, either in thought or in body. Therefore, I screen my thought-patterns for any unhealthy ideas, and I nullify any restrictions through daily identification and release. I begin anew each day to bless my body and see it in infant-like freshness. I delight in vigorous good health, and give thanks to the perfect Source from which it endlessly comes.

. . . According to your faith be it unto you.   —Matthew 9:29

SICKNESS IS NOT A SPIRITUAL REALITY; IT IS AN EXPERIENCE—AN EFFECT AND NOT A CAUSE.   —*The Science of Mind,* page 177

II

To Your Loves

L IFE WOULD surely be one-sided without some wonderful, durable human relationships, for these are your opportunities to love and be loved, to discover the complexities of human character in yourself and in others. Your human relationships tell you a great deal about yourself. As a wise person once suggested to me, they involve not so much having someone to *live* with as they do having someone to be *alive* with!

As with all other things, the quality of your friends and relationships is going to be determined by the quality of your ideas about yourself. Thus, these pages are written especially to help you uncover the ideas you have about relationships. You may see yourself represented as you already are . . . or you may discover areas where improvement seems appropriate. Whichever is the case, remember that Love—the essence of good relationships—is a quality which *is already present* in you. Love is natural for you, and if too many problems have been occurring when the chance to be loving appears in your life, the commentaries which follow may guide you toward some new understandings about the most loving, wonderful person you will ever know—*you!*

Here's to your Loves!

THREE LITTLE WORDS

"I LOVE YOU!" These eight little letters really pack a wallop, but that phrase is also probably one of the most ill-used in our language. It is just not understood.

Every time we are drawn physically to one of the opposite sex; every time we experience an airy, romantic feeling; every time we fall into a sentimental, nostalgic reverie, we find ourselves using the word "love" to describe what we have felt. But, considering what we know of love's Divine origin, we use the word very carelessly.

If, as the Bible says, we "dwell in God" when we love, should we not care enough to develop a vital understanding of what it means to love? We ought to realize that we make a commitment whenever we speak of love. In speaking of love for another, we commit ourselves through love to see, to touch, to experience the Divine Presence in that person. If we truly love another, what we actually feel is God, as Love, in that loved person. Real love, therefore, should give clarity to our lives, not cloudiness. Never can we be more Godlike than when we love another. So, when next you say "I love you" to another, be aware of what you have actually declared!

In Divine oneness I share the essence of Love with my dear ones. In mutual respect and enjoyment of this Divine Love for another, I grow in spiritual stature, letting no pettiness or temporary disagreement mar my vision of God's Presence in me or in them. I am grateful for the deep satisfaction that is found in this inner realization of true Love.

God is love; and he that dwelleth in love dwelleth in God. . . .
—I John 4:16

MY LOVE GOES OUT TO EVERY ONE IN THE WORLD; I DO NOT EXCLUDE ANYTHING, FOR I LOVE ALL NATURE AND EVERYTHING THAT IS.
—*The Science of Mind,* page 547

RIGHT RELATIONSHIPS

O UR TREATMENT of the people closest to us indicates what our own inner feelings are about ourselves. If we are secure within ourselves, sure of our inherent Divinity, and know that we have an irreplaceable part in the Divine plan, we will tend to be loving and understanding with our family and friends. We know that they, too, are expressions of Spirit even though they may, as Thoreau has written, "hear a different drummer."

When we feel confident in our spiritual knowledge, we will not thrust our own will upon those around us. Our enlightened spiritual consciousness will attract like-minded people into our lives. Our relationships will be spontaneous and joyful, capable of being developed into loving friendships. We cannot hope for enduring ties if we coerce our colleagues with narrow, limited consciousness; only in an expanded awareness can we live an expansive life. Let us begin now to allow our dear ones the greater freedom of their own infinite expression. We will enjoy better relationships than ever before.

I turn to the one Spirit that manifests in the limitless diversity of creation, and recognize this Spirit in everyone. I bless my family, friends, and colleagues; and I free them to their highest individual expression of Divinity. My friendships deepen with this expanded consciousness. Gone are the ties that bind me or restrict any of those who share my life. My relationships are relaxed, natural, and harmonious, for Divine understanding pervades all my dealings. I give thanks.

Now there are diversities of gifts, but the same Spirit. . . . And there are diversities of operations, but it is the same God which worketh all in all.
—I Corinthians 12:4, 6

THE ONE WHO HAS LEARNED TO LOVE ALL PEOPLE WILL FIND PLENTY OF PEOPLE WHO WILL RETURN THAT LOVE.
—*The Science of Mind*, page 297

21

A CURE FOR LONELINESS

"I AM WITH YOU . . . even unto the end of the world." These words of Jesus, while clearly meant to be comforting and loving, are often not fully understood. Because of their placement in the Bible, we might easily read them as being Jesus' promise that his resurrected presence would aid his disciples in their future work. But when we remind ourselves of how completely Jesus felt himself to be one with God, we can sense a much larger meaning in his statement.

If we believe there is only One Life, and Jesus' unity with that Life was total, then we shall know that Jesus was declaring a general truth about all life. He bore a message for mankind. It is not possible, he knew, for God to be separated from His Creation, for Creation could not exist for one moment without this union.

It is possible, however, for the creatures of this Creation to feel a *sense* of separation through confusion and misunderstanding. When this happens, our loneliness becomes unspeakable, but when we are aware of God's Presence and stay in right relation to It, we become filled with Life and all Its wonderful qualities. The feeling of separation and loneliness disappears.

There is only one life, God's Life, and I am one with It. **Knowing this, I never feel lonely, awkward, or confused. I am at ease wherever I am, for the Divine Presence guides me in what to say and do.**

I am Life's good instrument—vigorous, enthusiastic, and confident. I love being with others, and they, sensing this, are drawn to me. Thank you, Father, for a full life.

. . . lo, I am with you alway, even unto the end of the world.
—Matthew 28:20

THE UNITY OF GOOD IS A REVELATION OF THE GREATEST IMPORTANCE, FOR IT TEACHES US THAT WE ARE ONE WITH THE WHOLE AND ONE WITH EACH OTHER. —*The Science of Mind*, page 332

I FORGIVE MYSELF AS I FORGIVE OTHERS

WHEN ANOTHER person reacts to us unfavorably, we may be sure that we have evoked such a response because, consciously or unconsciously, we were caught up in a negative thought pattern. So if we would change another's attitude toward us, we might first make some changes in our own minds. Although others may be benefited as we consistently clarify our thoughts, the repair work need go on only in *our* minds.

We are usually our own worst enemy, weighting ourselves down with feelings like anger or guilt. This not only solves nothing, it also misdirects energy that could be put to constructive use. Defensive, resentful attitudes automatically demand "punishment" or unpleasantness from others, as surely as effect follows cause. Therefore, we can improve our relationships by examining and revising our own thought patterns. We actually can forgive ourselves by habitually substituting affirmative mental responses for negative ones; then the way is paved for us to forgive the real or imagined harm done to us by others.

I *know* I need to reckon only with today's needs and today's deeds. I do not set unrealistic expectations for myself or for others, but release concern about yesterday's mistakes. Infinite Intelligence alone knows what is in my heart and mind, and I let Its discerning influence erase any detrimental thought. Today I forgive myself as well as others for shortcomings, and go forth relieved of discord, so I am always in a right relationship to the Infinite.

And be ye kind one to another, tenderhearted, forgiving one another, even as God . . . hath forgiven you. —Ephesians 4:32

WE ARE TOLD THAT GOD WILL FORGIVE US *AFTER* WE HAVE FORGIVEN OTHERS. . . . IF GOD CAN WORK FOR US ONLY BY WORKING THROUGH US, THEN THIS . . . IS REALLY A STATEMENT OF THE LAW OF CAUSE AND EFFECT. —*The Science of Mind*, page 431

THE AWARENESS OF LOVE

LONELINESS is never greater than when it is experienced by people who believe they have no love in their lives. Such people often feel totally isolated, whether they are with others or not. They feel basically separated from life, from some essential part of themselves.

Ernest Holmes, speaking of Divine Love, called It an impelling force, a force not created *by* us but conducted *through* us. Since we are not originators of the force called Love, we can only be instruments of It, and in fact we *must* be. By Its nature, Love moves through us, on out into our world. If we cause It to remain uncirculated within us, throttled by fear or disdained because of past hurts, we risk the feelings of loneliness and separation that ensue, and the physical illnesses they might bring. Love is necessarily an active energy. If It is not shared, we feel fundamental discontent. For the sake of our well-being, Love must be allowed the freedom to energize us and to call forth Itself in others.

God is the Sublime Essence of Life, and because I am One with God, Life in Its fullness is mine. I welcome the power of Love within me. I accept Its outgoing nature and allow It to extend Itself through me, touching the lives of others. Divine Love in me calls to Itself in others. Therefore, I am never lonely, never afraid to love and be loved, always healthy and harmonized by Love.

. . . the fruit of the Spirit is love. . . . —Galatians 5:22

THE GREAT LOVE WHICH I NOW FEEL FOR THE WORLD IS THE LOVE OF GOD, AND IT IS FELT BY ALL AND COMES BACK TO ME FROM ALL.
—*The Science of Mind*, page 299

HOW TO LOVE TROUBLESOME PEOPLE

WE MAY FIND it a large order at times to follow Jesus' commandment to love one another. How can we love people we don't even like? It may be helpful, therefore, to remember that the bad-tempered person makes himself more miserable than the objects of his vituperative outbursts. He, more than anyone, needs the love from others that he is simply too self-involved to attract.

There is a kind of divine, impersonal Love which is ours to bestow upon all people. It is the Love of God acting through us that wishes everyone well, the Love that does not interfere with the growth of others nor make judgments based on outer appearances. Exercising this Divine Love, we can appreciate everyone as God's creations, recognizing their right to express Life as they will. We do not have to like what they do or be influenced by it.

Blessing these people as beloved by God, we can release them to their own good, thus opening a pathway for them either to pass from our lives or to join with us in a meeting of minds.

There is only one life, God's Life, and I am one with it. **I am a channel of God's Love. I am not negatively influenced by troubled appearances of others, for I steadfastly recognize them as beloved creations of the Most High.**

I am protected from all harmful opinions, since I am attuned only to Divine Direction. I bless all and release them to their good, thereby allowing them the fruit of their own expression.

He that loveth his brother abideth in the light, and there is none occasion of stumbling in him.
—I John 2:10

FROM SELFISH REASONS ALONE, IF FROM NO LOFTIER REASON, WE CANNOT AFFORD TO FIND FAULT, TO HATE, OR EVEN TO HOLD IN MIND *ANYTHING* AGAINST ANY LIVING SOUL.
—*The Science of Mind,* page 299

FORGIVE, FORGIVE, FORGIVE

THERE ARE few things that wreak more havoc on one's peace of mind than a person or circumstance crying out for forgiveness. We simply cannot afford *not* to forgive. When asked by Peter if he should forgive another seven times, Jesus answered, "Until seventy times seven," which implies continuous forgiveness. And, of course, he displayed the ultimate in forgiveness when he prayed for his tormentors from the cross.

Harbored hurts are breeding grounds for disease. They create dark, dank corners in the mind which fester until they outpicture as some unhealthy situation. If we find we are nurturing a resentment toward something or someone, we should immediately turn it over to God's Wisdom for dissolution. No dark thought can ever withstand the Light of Divine Love, if we truly let that Light in. By forgiveness we are released from that which made us unhappy, while in unforgiveness we remain in bondage to it, and it assumes an undeserved power in our lives. For our own growth, we must forgive until "seventy times seven" if necessary.

God is the Power of Love which purifies and cleanses my every thought. Through oneness with God every thought is worthwhile and deserving of my Divine awareness. I let no real or imagined hurt take root within me, and I turn to God for guidance in all my relationships. I bring only love. I expect only love in return. For this I give thanks.

And be ye kind one to another, tenderhearted, forgiving one another. . . .
—Ephesians 4:32

WE CANNOT AFFORD TO HOLD PERSONAL ANIMOSITIES OR ENMITIES AGAINST THE WORLD OR INDIVIDUAL MEMBERS OF SOCIETY.
—*The Science of Mind*, page 431

HOW TO LOVE SUCCESSFULLY

THE PERSON who could package and sell a surefire prescription for successful love relationships would become a millionaire overnight! Unfortunately, nobody seems to know how to do it.

But the wise one, Jesus, gave us a foolproof method in a single sentence, which we could apply to our lives at this moment if we chose. While speaking with his disciples during one of his last gatherings with them, he said, ". . . love one another as I have loved you." We are, he implied, to love others, whoever or whatever they may be. Jesus loved others as they were. He loved harlots, fishermen, tax collectors, fumblers, bumblers, people who fell asleep on the job—ordinary people. He saw in them, not the weaknesses, the inconsistencies, or the broken promises of human nature, but his kinship with them as other sons of the only Father.

We are all in the same boat, each of us on his way toward realizing a complete Oneness with God. Some seem to progress a little more quickly than others, so we might consider being a little less demanding, a little less critical, a little more Godlike in our loving.

God is pure Love, flowing throughout all Life, throughout me. I see people as God made them, loving and lovable, and I am not dismayed by any apparent lack of perfection which may appear. I am concerned only with their Divine nature, and this is what I call forth. We are all brothers in spirit, doing our best at the moment.

This is my commandment, That ye love one another, as I have loved you.
—John 15:12

LOVE IS GREATER THAN ALL ELSE AND COVERS A MULTITUDE OF MISTAKES. —*The Science of Mind,* page 504

THOU SHALT LOVE

W E ALL KNOW of Jesus' two great commandments for living a good life. One was to love God completely, and the other was to love our neighbors. To students of Truth, the idea of loving God completely means more than to have mere sentimental thoughts of affection about a deity. To love God is to become as aware as possible of our Oneness with God, thereby making us instruments of God's Love, able to express that love to others. We become true lovers of life in the greatest sense of the word.

It is not enough to love the few "neighbors" whom we contact during each day. We need to enhance the quality of everybody's life by the enlightened quality of our thoughts, our work, and our service. Then we stop becoming part of life's problems and begin to become part of its answers. This is loving in the greatest and dearest sense, for in this way we can touch our neighbors universally.

God is perfect Life, and this Life moves through me progressively as inspiration, thought, and action. I know that God and I are One, inseparable, and this knowledge frees me from fear, anxiety, and frustration. I move easily through all my activities with thoughts of loving awareness. I naturally enhance my own life, the lives of my immediate neighbors, and life on the cosmic scale; and I am thankful that everything I do brings forth good.

. . . Thou shalt love the Lord thy God with all thy heart, and with all thy soul, and with all thy mind. . . . Thou shalt love thy neighbour as thyself.
—Matthew 22:37, 39

LOVE IS A COMPLETE UNITY WITH LIFE, AND WE CANNOT ENTER THIS STATE UNLESS WE ARE IN UNITY WITH ALL THAT LIVES, FOR ALL LIFE IS ONE. —*The Science of Mind*, page 459

THE ART OF PEOPLESHIP

WHEN WE learn of the *I Am* within ourselves, we glory in It and perhaps concentrate much attention on Its growth. But we, like everyone else, can be guilty of forgetting that the *I Am* quality in others is just as dear to God as is our own. It must be that we forget how precious people really are or we would not do and say thoughtless, noninspired things to one another.

People do not move about in squads or platoons. They cannot be categorized like so many pieces of fruit. People go about singly, individually, and they are constantly expressing the Divine Spirit in the best ways they know how.

There is often an aura of "bigness" to our lives—big governments, big supermarkets, big cars—and it can tend to minimize the individual's worth in his own eyes. Perhaps we should concentrate on doing fewer things but doing them better and with as much personal concern as possible. We contain the kingdom of God right where we are!

God is Life, **and in that Life we are all sustained. As priceless as my life is to the infinite Presence, I know that the individual expressions of others are just as dear.**

We are all begotten of the only Father.

Today, I consider the personal needs and desires of all who are in my world and I extend to them the invitation to grow with me in personal, spiritual advancement through the power of a grateful heart.

But even the very hairs of your head are all numbered. Fear not therefore. . . .
                                                        —Luke 12:7

IN EACH ONE OF US, TO EACH ONE OF US, THROUGH EACH ONE OF US, SOMETHING IS PERSONALIZED. . . .   —*The Science of Mind,* page 89

LOVE THY NEIGHBOR

IN MANY OF the New Testament books, we are admonished to love our neighbors, the following of which noble admonition is downright essential to successful life. Often though, the ways in which we should love others are not clear. Then, when we discover Ernest Holmes' idea that Love is the "self-givingness of Spirit," we recognize that Love is more than an affectionate attachment to others. Love is the universal impetus that Life Itself has, to be about the business of living!

We are to look past the limited interpretation of Love, then, and know that It is more than just being "in love" with someone. We must love the right of others to express themselves, and we must learn to love these many expressions. If we do not, we are thwarting the "givingness" of Life in Its flow through us and in our response to It in others.

Our love of others must totally exclude hostile ideas regarding people in general or in particular, for hostility obstructs Love's course through us.

God *is Love*, and in the stronghold of Love I eternally abide.

Through Love, I appreciate the special qualities of others, releasing all suspicions and enmities which may hinder Love's course. In a constructive fashion I acknowledge the right of others to express themselves in their own particular ways.

I recognize the Divinity in others and love It, seeing only the good and the lovable in them.

. . . Thou shalt love thy neighbour as thyself.   —Matthew 19:19

LOVE IS SELF-GIVINGNESS THROUGH CREATION, THE IMPARTATION OF THE DIVINE THROUGH THE HUMAN.

—*The Science of Mind*, page 478

SUCCESSFUL HUMAN RELATIONS

Happy and fulfilling relationships are not only desirable for a balanced life, they are necessary! And if we want to attract love into our lives, we know that first we must be loving. Thus, love will be attracted to us by the universal law of Cause and Effect.

Those who are drawn to us must be allowed to respond to us in their own way. Once we trust the Divine Presence to bring loving companions into our lives, we must rely upon It to assure that those people will be like-minded, people who will add their own wonderful touches to our lives while benefiting from the good we have to give them.

To have enduring relationships, we must embody in ourselves the qualities we wish to see in our friends—honesty, loyalty, sincerity, compassion, loving concern—and all the other qualities that lift our lives out of a state of bare existence and fill them with Divine meaning.

In giving the best of ourselves, we will call forth the best in our friends.

God in me manifests as a person of the highest caliber, for I concentrate my attention on becoming the best possible example of Divine qualities. Wonderful, loving people are attracted to me, and I give the best of myself to them . . . lovingly, openly, and with honesty. And I expect a like response from them. I give thanks for blessed human relationships.

He that loveth his brother abideth in the light, and there is none occasion of stumbling in him.
—I John 2:10

Like attracts like and it is also true that we may become attracted to something which is greater than our previous experience, by first embodying the atmosphere of our desire.
—*The Science of Mind*, page 294

GOD'S UNSPEAKABLE LOVE

WE HAVE learned, in the more sensitive phases of our development, to become acutely aware of the feelings of those about us by simply observing the movements and positions of their bodies—a kind of nonverbal form of communication commonly referred to as "body language." How many times, for example, is talk unnecessary between those who love each other! It is enough to be near a loved one and to sense the unspoken communication always taking place between like-natured souls.

God's Love in man is expressed in many ways. It is revealed by the artist through the spoken and written word, or with paint brush and canvas. But equally wonderful is that aspect of Love which often cannot be fully objectified, but only sensed. We may feel It when our emotions are aroused by listening to beautiful music, by observing a lovely sunset, or by watching small children at play. And through prayer and meditation we may intuitively sense this Love even more perfectly, more completely!

I am aware of the deep universal Love that underlies all creation. I see this Love in nature's beautiful, orderly form and function, and I sense It in a thrilling, intuitive way as It unites me with all things and with all life. I lift up my whole thought to the influx of God's Love and accept the creative direction of Its inspiration. Thank you, Father.

I love them that love me; and those that seek me early shall find me.
—Proverbs 8:17

THE LOVE OF GOD BINDS ME TO ITSELF, AND WILL NOT LET ME GO.
—*The Science of Mind*, page 513

THE PERFECT LOVE

IT IS HARD for the average person to realize how perfectly God loves His Creation. Perhaps we may understand such Love a little more if we look at our own love relationships. Do our true friends cease to love us even when we are less than our best selves? Are our enduring relationships built only upon good times, fading away when hard times come along? The answers to these questions are, of course, no. And when we realize that *this* is love *imperfectly* interpreted, fraught with human ups-and-downs and limitation, we get an idea of how wonderful Love is at Its origin.

God cannot *not* love us, for the nature of the Divine is to go forth into Creation and never to retract Itself. So we may count on Love's constructive purpose for us as It works through us. We, by our lack of understanding, may appear to thwart Love's course, but not for long. The Universal Love, lawfully and predictably, makes Itself known to us every time we are open to receive It. Thus do we come to know, more perfectly, perfect Love in action.

I am one with God's perfect Love.

I see It in action daily in the cycle of life around me. It refines Itself in me and in all people, everywhere. I know that God's purpose for me is only good, always munificent. I trust Divine Love in me to interpret Itself perfectly in all my activities, and I let this Love go forth from me as It must.

I am grateful that Love can never leave me, never fail to guide me in every right way.

. . . the God of love and peace shall be with you. —II Corinthians 13:11

LOVE IS THE IMPELLING FORCE AND LAW EXECUTES THE WILL OF LOVE.
—*The Science of Mind,* page 323

FRIENDSHIP

NO ONE AMONG us doubts the value of sincere friends. Drawn to us to share our joys and cares, our friends seem to be the answer to that inner plea, "Father, I want to touch You in some way." And our friends are, indeed, a bit of God in form. More than just a joy, friends are the mirrors that Life puts up so we may see ourselves, for we draw to us those people who are like us in nature and in consciousness.

They will be varied, of course, as our own interests are many and varied, but they will generally reflect some aspect of our own outlook on Life. If we are loving and giving, they will have these qualities. If, however, we find that our friends are rather critical, gossipy, or tightminded, we may have to admit that these are some qualities we are exhibiting ourselves. Let us look for a moment at these close-ups to determine if we are happy with what we see. If we aren't, criticism of our friends won't solve anything. What we must do is seek more compassion and understanding within ourselves, and thus attract to us those persons who embody a similar compassion and understanding.

God, the only Life there is, and I are joyously one. I give thanks for treasured friends, and from them I learn great lessons about myself. I commune with the Divine Presence daily so I may make God's ways my own. In doing so, I draw to myself inspired companions, with whom I may happily share life along the pathway of spiritual discovery. I look for God in others.

Wherefore comfort yourselves together, and edify one another, even as also ye do. —I Thessalonians 5:11

THE ONE WHO HAS LEARNED TO LOVE ALL PEOPLE WILL FIND PLENTY OF PEOPLE WHO WILL RETURN THAT LOVE. —*The Science of Mind*, page 297

III

To Your True Expression

THERE ARE some very nice people around who are actually living false identities. They are living lives that belong to other people . . . people whose opinions and desires have become the guiding force of their own lives. If these forces were suddenly removed, they would no longer know how to conduct themselves. They would have to reestablish their identities. There are also those people who are crammed into niches that simply don't fit them, but who grumpily stay there wondering if that's all life has to offer.

The readings on the coming pages are for those of you who are suffering from a crimp in your expression, those of you who know there is more to life than what you are doing right now.

You have always been a wellspring of endless talents, but many of them lie undiscovered. Your mind recognizes and knows what you can do, and will tell you so if you will let it. Let the following ideas help you to discover your hidden talents and make them work for you. If you have been filling someone else's shoes, it is time for you to step out on your own . . . in your own shoes!

Here's to your True Expression!

DO IT NOW!

IS THERE A dream you have been hiding in your heart? A project you have been putting off? Some creative endeavor that you seem never to get around to? Why not resolve today to act upon these creative impulses, for they are the urgings of Spirit within you, which ever desires to thrust Itself into expression through you. When these urges go unheeded, your energies are either dissipated in unproductive ways, or they turn inward, creating frustrations that make you restless and dissatisfied with life.

How to bring these energies into play? How to release them? Affirmative prayer is one way, for it is a method by which you see your desires being fulfilled *right now*. And if you can't create a powerful image of your desires being fulfilled in this moment, perhaps that is a clue to what the problem is. Perhaps you haven't truly committed yourself to having what you desire, and Law is just reflecting your indecision. Do decisions need to be made? Then make them now, and let Spirit express through you!

I know that God's Spirit within me is the Source of my being. My life's purpose is to let It express through me in the form of good and creative acts. God knows nothing of delay or incompleteness; therefore, now is the time for me to fulfill my creative impulses. I feel a great satisfaction as I set in motion projects long set aside, and let Divine Wisdom guide me toward their constructive completion. My endeavors are blessed, as creative energies flow into that which I can and should perform. They bring good to me and to others. Right now, I gratefully accept the right fulfillment of my dreams and goals.

Therefore I say unto you, What things soever ye desire, when ye pray, believe that ye receive them, and ye shall have them. —Mark 11:24

THE TIME HAS COME, THE HOUR HAS STRUCK. THE POWER FROM WITHIN HAS COME FORTH AND IS EXPRESSING THROUGH MY WORD. I DO NOT HAVE TO WAIT; TODAY IS THE TIME.

—*The Science of Mind*, page 520

STEP OUT OF CONDITIONING

W E ARE A combination of all the thoughts we have ever thought about ourselves, and these thoughts have probably been influenced by others almost all of our lives. We are affected by the environment around us. We respond to the opinions of others. We, like a mirror, reflect the comings and goings of circumstances in general, and those circumstances are often disconnected, disquieting, and discouraging.

We need to become aware of the fact that we began life as sovereign, individualized particles of the Divine Presence, and that our ability to think consciously was the door by which we were intended to gain entrance to the perfect world of Spirit, which is meant to be ours. Knowing this, we can now begin to step away from the conditioned ideas we may have about ourselves, no matter how negative they are. Since we are of Divine Stuff, our background is of the best, no matter what we have been taught to the contrary. We are heirs to God's Kingdom, and we should view ourselves accordingly. As children of the King, we can have the cream of life if we are willing to accept it.

As the perfect Life is my life, I now accept myself for what I am—heir to the riches of the inner Kingdom of peace, poise, harmony, and success.

I expect the best in life, and I know I am worthy of it. I am no longer subject to past negative conditioning, and I am free from the opinions of others.

I move forward on my own, subject only to the direction of the presence of Life within me.

Wherefore thou art no more a servant, but a son; and if a son, then an heir of God through Christ. —Galatians 4:7

THE INNER SPIRIT, WHICH IS GOD, BEARS WITNESS TO THE DIVINE FACT THAT WE ARE THE SONS OF GOD, THE CHILDREN OF THE MOST HIGH.
—*The Science of Mind*, page 485

I VISUALIZE MY DESIRES

THE GIFT OF imagination is one of the most powerful of God's blessings. By using it properly, we can effectively control the workings of the subjective part of life for our enormous benefit. Ernest Holmes tells us that the subjective, or Law, is "the servant of the Eternal Spirit throughout all the ages." It is able to return to us only what we think into It, and all we put into It registers, especially the vivid picture-images. For many of us, in fact, picturing our desires carries a stronger conviction than just words alone. It helps to clarify the subjective state of our consciousness and makes clearer to us what we actually want.

Do we want a healthy body? Let us envision ourselves mentally upright, strong, energetic in every limb. Do we want a new home? Let us see ourselves going from room to room, placing in it every feature we desire. We must be diligent in our imaginative work and focus our attention upon the objects we want to bring into our experience. Law needs a clear picture to work with. The old saying, "One picture is worth a thousand words," could not have more meaning than in the affirmative directing of Mind-Power.

I *know* that universal Mind already contains perfect good. Today I seek to realize this fully, and keep my mind on the good I desire, so it may be fulfilled. Without becoming tense or anxious, I envision my desire now as an already accomplished fact, presented to me in a way that is completely right and in harmony with my total well-being. I keep my mind clear and untroubled so the picture I project will be sharp and definite. I enter gratefully into the joy of its presence . . . now.

Where there is no vision, the people perish: but he that keepeth the law, happy is he.   —Proverbs 29:18

TO EACH, LIFE BRINGS THE REWARD OF HIS OWN VISIONING. . . .
                                          —*The Science of Mind*, page 442

I ACCEPT CHANGE

WE KNOW that God works as a constantly changing medium. Ernest Holmes tells us that God is the great Unformed, expressing Itself in form. As soon as one life-form serves its purpose, it is put aside for another, more suitable one. We see this in earth's revolving seasons, and even in the discarding of our bodies when we no longer need them. Change is a great refresher; it sweeps away what is outmoded and makes way for new, wider vistas. We are creatures fully equipped for everlasting readjustment. If this were not so, there would never have been a single new invention since the dawn of history.

We should remember that change does not mean loss. Change is the outward manifestation of an inward rise in consciousness! It may mean a move to a new city or a new occupation, and this is God's way of placing us in a position we have grown to deserve. We need to keep our thinking flexible, free from fear and tension, so we may recognize God's opportunity when it comes to us. We are never placed in circumstances that are not opportunities for growth.

I *know* that in the Mind of God there is a plan, a purpose, a suitable place that I can fill. Divine Mind contains myriad forms and expressions that are constantly being discovered by man. I am a part of this Divine unfoldment. I offer no resistance to the flood of energy at work in me, bringing more life to me, though it may initially require from me more attention to disciplined thinking. I trust that infinite Intelligence knows what is best for me, and I am ready to make any change necessary.

And he changeth the times and the seasons: he removeth kings, and setteth up kings: he giveth wisdom unto the wise, and knowledge to them that know understanding. . . . —Daniel 2:21

SPIRIT IS NEVER BOUND BY THE FORM IT TAKES, AND IS NOT AFFECTED BY ANY APPARENT CAUSE OR CONDITION, BUT IS FOREVER FREE.
—*The Science of Mind*, page 184

I SHARE MY GOOD

KIND WORDS and deeds tap into a marvelous realm of creativity. Eric Hoffer, the author, gives a wonderful example. As a young man in Depression days, he picked peas for a small wage, and at the end of one particular day, his last basket was not quite full. So he started back through the rows, hoping to find enough peas to fill it. At the opposite end of the rows another man started picking peas and filling his hat with them, much to the author's disgust. When he reached Mr. Hoffer, the man dumped his peas into Eric's basket and exclaimed, "Now, you owe someone else a hatful of peas!"

Others may need the special good we have to give. Perhaps a word of praise for someone's efforts would help that person recognize the Divine intent in himself. In everyone there is a spiritual expression we can sense and compliment. As we grow in Divine enlightenment, we will naturally want to share our spiritual benefits with others, since many hands have helped us along our own path of spiritual unfoldment. We, in turn, owe our love and encouragement to those who are also looking for understanding.

I *know* God works in wonderful ways to bring forth my good, and I bless all who have been instrumental in its manifestation—strangers, friends, and loved ones. I remember when I have been helped by others and there was no opportunity to return the favor, times when others were not even aware of the beneficial influence they had upon my life. I live the Divine Life that is my intrinsic nature as fully as I can, so I may pass on these blessings, and I am eagerly attentive to the God-being in everyone I meet.

But to do good and to communicate forget not: for with such sacrifices God is well pleased. —Hebrews 13:16

THERE IS ALWAYS MORE GOOD THAN BAD IN PEOPLE, AND SEEING THE GOOD TENDS TO BRING IT FORTH. LOVE IS THE GRANDEST HEALING AND DRAWING POWER ON EARTH. —*The Science of Mind,* page 298

FEELING IS THE SECRET

EXPERIENCED metaphysicians know that the form in which a prayer is given is not what makes it effective. An enlightened affirmative prayer is a tremendous psychological aid, but the *feelings* attendant to prayer work carry the power. Many people know this and are forever seeking that magical surge of emotion which will envelop them and almost lift them off the ground. If it does not come, they are disappointed.

It is a mistake, however, to think that all prayer work must be accompanied with great starbursts of feeling. There will be times when such high emotion is present; but more often, effective prayer contains a simple sense of *knowing* which quietly steals through one's being, a sense that dictates, "All is well," in the midst of turmoil. This, too, is feeling—powerful, steadfast, unshakable . . . and it gets results. Such a sublime feeling is more predictable because we can call it into action more easily when we pray than we can a rapturous emotional state.

God is the Sublime Essence of Life, and because I am One with God, Life in Its fullness is mine. I am secure in my prayer work because I have great depth of feeling within me. I know the words I speak are true because I am filled with assurance. I enjoy my lofty flights of feeling, and I also give thanks for the continual, quiet movements of Spirit within me.

At that day ye shall know that I am in my Father, and ye in me, and I in you.   —John 14:20

WORDS CARRY THE MIND FORWARD TO A PLACE IN THOUGHT WHERE REALIZATION BEGINS.   —*The Science of Mind,* page 409

THE RISK OF BLOSSOMING

R ECENTLY, A wonderful bit of wisdom came to me
through a friend. In its glorious simplicity it read, "And
the day came when the risk to remain closed in a bud became
more painful than the risk it took to blossom." How
beautifully these words sum up our hesitancy to open toward
the new!

Indeed, there is risk in looking toward the unknown. All
expansion—whether spiritual, mental, emotional, or physical
—takes great faith and courage. Remaining where we are,
even if circumstances are not to our liking, often seems to be
simpler and safer . . . though there may arise some pain if we
consistently disregard the inner Divine Spark which says,
"Let Me fulfill you."

To all of us, though, there comes the day when we must
blossom, when to remain closed would put us in a kind of
mental peril. We *can* enjoy the fruits of the Spirit within us
and smell the fragrance of the blooms of Wisdom, Love,
Understanding, and Peace. Let us invite this spiritual unfoldment and cease fearing where it may take us.

**God is the Sublime Essence of Life, and because I am One
with God, Life in Its fullness is mine. I am alert to my
spiritual good. Because I trust, I know I can only receive
positive results from my spiritual search. I am unafraid. I accept the best, the happiest, the most creative and loving *me*
that I can be. I blossom forth to live a wondrous life, for I am
no longer content to remain in the bud.**

---

*If ye abide in me, and my words abide in you, ye shall ask what ye will,
and it shall be done unto you.*   —John 15:7

WITHIN EACH ONE OF US IS AN INDESTRUCTIBLE, AN ETERNAL, GOD-
INTENDED MAN, A PERFECT BEING . . . OUR PERFECT BEING.
                                              —*The Science of Mind,* page 338

CLIMB OUT OF THE PIT

O UR DIVINE inner nature is at all times harmonious, joyous, and undisturbed—a condition we would always enjoy on the outer level if we were properly attuned to God. But an aspect of our personality is susceptible to the alluring sights and sounds of earthly circumstances, sometimes to our great distraction and vexation.

It is not uncommon, then, for us to be torn and fearful, like the biblical father of old, so desirous of believing in only the best that life has to offer, yet caught up in the unbelief created by appearances. But despair and depression must not be allowed to have unchallenged dominion in our minds, for they become habit patterns of the most constricting kind. The instant we find ourselves temporarily in a mental pit, we must search out and exercise the boldest, most vigorous affirmation we know and speak it until words and feeling begin to correspond. God always responds!

I am uplifted and inspired by the Life of God as It unfolds and expands Itself through me this day. Nothing can upset me nor topple me from this expanded awareness. I am meant to experience the good things of life; therefore, temporary setbacks do not discourage me. I am guided by Infinite Intelligence and I let It lead me to ever greater good. With deep thanksgiving I accept happiness and joy, right now!

. . . Lord, I believe; help thou mine unbelief. —Mark 9:24

NO MATTER WHAT OUR EMOTIONAL STORM, OR WHAT OUR OBJECTIVE SITUATION MAY BE, THERE IS ALWAYS A SOMETHING HIDDEN IN THE INNER BEING THAT HAS NEVER BEEN VIOLATED.

—*The Science of Mind,* page 33

APPRECIATE YOURSELF

WE ARE taught that we are Divine in origin, that we spring from a perfect God, and that we are the beloved of our God. We must also realize that we come cloaked with our own individual nature, our brand of humanhood. We are wise therefore to know and understand this nature of ours and use it to our best advantage. We ought not waste time and energy wishing to be like someone else. Certainly we can emulate particular good qualities we find in others, but we surely cannot *be* someone else.

Should we not want to be different? All types of personalities combine to give life its flair, whereas so much dissatisfaction comes from our longing to be like another person, as if that would make our problems disappear. No, indeed, it will not. We can only start where we stand . . . knowing we are a specialized part of God, wisely appreciating who we are, what we can do, and glorying in the Divine Life we represent.

I am an emanation of the creative Presence, wonderful in my own right.

I am completely equipped to express Life fully, joyously, without restraint. I envy no one his talents, for my own excellence is necessary to Life.

I appreciate myself as I appreciate the contributions of others, and I cease to waste time in idle wishfulness. As God lives, I live—as an instrument of beauty, love, and creativity.

I am grateful to be me!

. . . I had planted thee a noble vine, wholly a right seed. . . .
—Jeremiah 2:21

WHAT A MAN HAS AND WHAT HE IS, IS THE RESULT OF THE SUBJECTIVE STATE OF HIS THOUGHT. —*The Science of Mind,* page 304

LOVE GOD AND LIVE IT UP!

A FINE TEACHER once said that we should love God and live it up! Probably the first thought that would come into the minds of many would be, "How?" Somehow we seem to have a hard time reconciling thoughts of God with ideas of a life of fullness, experience, and vigor. "Living it up," however, does not have to mean doing things we'll eventually have to live *down!*

If we could only realize that the Divine Life includes within It all we could possibly imagine in full daily living, we would not hesitate a moment in turning our lives over to God. Under Divine guidance, we would be open to experience new ideas and situations all the time, for stagnation is unknown to God. Besides that, we would be less inclined to run afoul of ourselves while engaging in the live-it-up cycle!

God's Life in us is joyous and eager, ever vital, ever curious. To love that Life invites living it up in the happiest possible way. Besides, to express Life to Its fullest is surely one of the reasons why we were created!

There is one Life, and It is Joy, Vigor, Enthusiasm, and Eagerness. This is the Divine Life of God, and I am one with Its capacity for happy self-expression.

I am open to all that Life teaches, and my experiences are fruitful. Under God's guidance, I am protected from unsuitable choices and from harmful, outer influences while I grow and learn. Life becomes more inviting and exciting by the day, and I am grateful to be on earth at this moment.

. . . let them also that love thy name be joyful in thee.　　—Psalm 5:11

LOVE IS THE SOLE IMPULSE FOR CREATION, AND THE MAN WHO DOES NOT HAVE LOVE AS THE GREATEST INCENTIVE IN HIS LIFE, HAS NEVER DEVELOPED THE REAL CREATIVE INSTINCT.

—*The Science of Mind*, page 298

EXPERT USE OF TIME AND TALENTS

WE ALL HAVE numerous interests, but few of us consider ourselves to be experts in many fields. Perhaps that is because the world shows us such a multitude of things to investigate that we tend to scatter our forces here and there: we dart like the butterfly from one interesting blossom of knowledge to another. It is vital to be interested, of course, but in time we may become dissatisfied if we find that we are a jack-of-all-trades and master of none.

To become an expert, we must cull out the more irrelevant pleasures and apply ourselves directly to one or two pursuits. We must spend time and energy advancing our knowledge and practice in these few, selected areas. If such concentration appears to be hard, we need only remember that Divine Mind stands ready to equip us with whatever we need—time, opportunity, teachers, etc. On our part, we must provide the *desire* to be so fulfilled. While God provides everything necessary for our fulfillment, He cannot provide individual motivation. As choice-making creatures, the will belongs to us. The way belongs to God.

God, the only Life there is, and I are joyously one. I willingly accept the all-wise guidance of God in my chosen fields of endeavor. I am led to everything I need in outer circumstances, while I eagerly provide desire on the inner level. My life is balanced. I know when to work, when to play, and when to rest, and I gratefully give thanks for a creative life of fulfillment.

But the manifestation of the Spirit is given to every man to profit withal.
—I Corinthians 12:7

THERE IS A LAW OF UNFOLDMENT IN MAN, WHICH SAYS HE CAN ADVANCE ONLY BY GOING FROM WHERE HE IS TO THE PLACE WHERE HE WOULD LIKE TO BE. —*The Science of Mind*, page 271

I AM A WINNER

WHAT MAKES the difference between a winner and a loser? Are people on the "winning side" some unique breed to whom heaven has given special gifts denied to others? We who study scientific spirituality know this cannot be true. The universe does not whimsically dole out favors to one and withhold them from another.

Using the simplest generalities, let us suggest that winners are inclined to go their own creative ways, while losers tend to be held in check by the influence and opinion of others. Winners march to an Inner Instruction and so seem to be freer from negative, disapproving comments of those around them. This characteristic manifests as strength and assurance, which is bound to produce results. Being constricted by fears of "what others will think," however, freezes the creative process, which leads to stagnation.

As we evolve, we will experience ups and downs. They are inseparable from growth. Our true concern must be, therefore, always to work in harmonious accord with the God-Presence in us, for in living a God-guided life, we shall know that what we do is in line with Divine will. And *that* is being a winner!

There is only one life, God's Life, and I am one with It. I am happily determined to live a buoyant, constructive, Divinely directed life—the life God intends me to have. I am, therefore, unaffected by the comments and opinions of others.

I depend only upon God, and I follow the dictates of Divine Conscience within me. I encourage others in their expression and gratefully accept my own.

My soul, wait thou only upon God; for my expectation is from him.
—Psalm 62:5

IN GLADNESS, THEN, WE SHOULD MAKE KNOWN OUR DESIRES, AND IN CONFIDENCE WE SHOULD WAIT UPON THE PERFECT LAW TO MANIFEST THROUGH US.
—*The Science of Mind*, page 272

LET'S GO!

THE EARTH IS a plane of action and activity, a place where needs and desires are met and filled every day. It is a place which demands vigorous, imaginative use of our time, talent, and energies. The student of Truth knows that through the Mind of God, all necessary knowledge is accessible to us. Through daily prayer and meditation we can tap the universe for its intelligence and its strength.

But wisdom and knowledge not put to active use benefit no one, so there comes a time when we must act and put what we know to the test. Although we may not always see clearly the ways by which we shall arrive at our goal, let's take that first step, trusting God to make straight our way as we go along. Are we, at times, a little afraid or insecure about our abilities? It is truly a courageous person who goes ahead with his plan even in the face of fear and doubt. Remember that we are promised the support of the Divine Companion whenever our courage begins to wane. Life needs us, our dreams, our contributions, our uniqueness. Let's go!

God as Cosmic Consciousness is forever creating and going forth. Through oneness with God I now become the recipient of this creative movement. I am filled with ideas, imbued with enthusiasm and sparked with the courage to turn my ideas into form. All my projects are preceded by prayer and silent meditation, so my acts are rightly channeled.

. . . for there is a time there for every purpose and for every work.
—Ecclesiastes 3:17

MAN ALONE IS ABLE TO CONSCIOUSLY WORK OUT HIS OWN DESTINY, TO DETERMINE WHAT MANNER OF LIFE HE SHALL LEAD.
—*The Science of Mind*, page 391

THE MATURE PERSON

THERE ARE perhaps fewer accomplishments greater than the one of acquiring maturity; everyone wants to be wise and well balanced in every area of his life. So let us see what some of the characteristics of maturity are. Strangely enough, we can begin by recognizing what maturity is *not*—and that is the simple attainment of age alone. For not every person of years is well matured.

The Bible tells us there is a time to put away childish things, which does not mean we should cease enjoying our open-hearted delights in life and other people. It does mean that our inner growth on the intellectual and emotional level should be in balance. All thought and no feeling makes a dull person, but runaway emotional reactions make an unruly child—at any age.

Perhaps one of the greatest signs of maturity comes when a person realizes he is incomplete without a knowledge and loving use of the Creative Presence. Such knowledge gives built-in guidance on how to respond to every circumstance—neither too vigorously nor too indifferently; it gives a sense of belonging to one's better Self . . . which is true maturity.

God is complete and total wisdom, and can never be at odds with Himself or Creation. I am free from extreme reactions, free from feelings beyond my control. I love and enjoy life. I know, through Infinite Guidance, that I am capable of living a mature, fulfilling life.

When I was a child, I spake as a child, I understood as a child, I thought as a child: but when I became a man, I put away childish things.
—I Corinthians 13:11

MAN'S MIND IS THE MIND OF GOD FUNCTIONING AT THE LEVEL OF MAN'S UNDERSTANDING OF HIS PLACE IN THE UNIVERSE.
—*The Science of Mind*, page 394

YOUR INNER SUPPORT SYSTEM

IT IS QUITE popular these days to contemplate all the things in our lives that we have going for us and call them our "support system." This may include our position in life, our loved ones, and our possessions; but the most durable support system is the one which cannot be seen or experienced objectively. It is an undergirding which comes from our inner selves and involves intangibles that are unique to each person.

And just what is our personal foundation? Is it a liveable philosophy that we turn to every day? Does it make us secure and stable enough in all our beliefs, so we truly live and let live? Does it allow us happily to enjoy our lives in the most enlightened way we can . . . and allow others the freedom to do the same?

If we answer, "Yes!" to these questions, we know we have a life which can be secure from disruptive influences. And as we daily learn to depend more and more on our inner support system, basing our lives completely on this spiritual foundation, we will find all of our deepest longings satisfied.

God is perfect Life, and this Life moves through me progressively as inspiration, thought, and action. I know God is the only force at work within life. This force is perfectly good, always flexible in its response to me, and always available to me. I am secure in such knowledge. Outer appearances and the opinions of others cannot disturb my trust in God's wisdom and guidance. I thankfully turn to God for daily support.

My voice shalt thou hear in the morning, O Lord; in the morning will I direct my prayer unto thee, and will look up. —Psalm 5:3

THE SPIRIT WITHIN MAN IS GOD, AND ONLY TO THE DEGREE THAT WE LISTEN TO AND SEEK TO OBEY THIS SPIRIT SHALL WE REALLY SUCCEED.
—*The Science of Mind,* page 275

IV

To Your Prosperity

I F YOU FEEL you will be a better person by not having the good things in life, you might consider skipping this section. If, however, you believe you can have it all, then read on.

Nothing is too good to be true, and nothing is too much for you to have if you believe you can have it. Many people live prosperous, successful lives because they have faith in themselves and in their abilities. Others, however, have allowed a string of failures to get them down. They let their minds be shaped by what they see around them and by what other people say. They do not know that they, and not other people and circumstances, are the directors of their lives.

The following pages are dedicated to the idea that you can bring prosperity into your life by first bringing it into your mind. There are many ways here to help you think more richly. What better time is there than now for you to begin to have more money and to enjoy good things? What better time is there than now for you to change your mind about your living conditions and accept better ones? I commend these readings to you for this richer, fuller life.

Here's to your Prosperity!

51

RIGHT CIRCULATION

THE LAW OF circulation is an important one, in both our objective and subjective lives. When ideas grow static and attitudes immovable, we tend to experience a lack of circulation in our physical lives. Unity writer Catherine Ponder says, "Basically there is only one disease, congestion. And there is only one cure, circulation." When our thoughts become congested and not open to the fluidity of free movement, our bodies will eventually show this inactivity. Some organ or channel will cease to let Life flow freely through it. We may see this occur in money matters as well. If our thoughts about money are closed on one end, we cannot experience the circulation of abundance in our lives.

If Ms. Ponder is correct in saying that the only cure is circulation, our answer is obvious. We need to become better conductors of Life. We have to be open on both ends. We must be givers to become receivers. Good must go forth from us if Life—which includes money—is to come to us. In this way, we keep Life moving through us. Mentally, as we expand our awareness to take in new insights, we shall also reap a physical bounty of greater health and abundance.

God is the Sublime Essence of Life, and because I am One with God, Life in Its fullness is mine. Peaceful thoughts, healthy thoughts, prosperous thoughts flow through me freely, and I experience an increase of peace, good health, and financial abundance in my circumstances. I am open to inspiration and Divine instruction. Thus, good circulates throughout my life in every way.

. . . the inward man is renewed day by day. —II Corinthians 4:16

IT IS ONLY AS WE ALLOW THE DIVINE CURRENT TO FLOW THROUGH US ON AND OUT, THAT WE REALLY EXPRESS LIFE.

—*The Science of Mind,* page 440

THE AWARENESS OF MONEY

MONEY IS A good thing. Money is part of God's Good coming to us in a specialized form. Therefore, we are not selfish or unspiritual to pray for money. We do not, after all, have to consider taking away someone else's money, for we are merely drawing to us that which is our own to have.

Somehow, many people never seem to have as much money as they would like, and there could be several reasons for this. They might not feel they are worth much; perhaps they regard having more money only as wishful thinking, and they may not be ready to make use of greater sums of money.

If we want to prosper greatly, we can accept money from numerous sources, not just from specified areas. We must not be afraid of the increased responsibility that having more money brings, either, for that goes with the territory. We are worth every dollar that comes to us. And we must also remember to be grateful to our spiritual Source both mentally and financially; for our financial seed, returned to God's work in some way, assures us of further good harvest.

God is the Sublime Essence of Life, and because I am One with God, Life in Its fullness is mine. I am rich, both in spiritual wisdom and in physical resources. I give thanks for my increased good in the form of money, and I am grateful for guidance in its proper use. There is no negative concern in me about money, for I regard it as part of God's means of sustaining me. I bless my spiritual sources, as I am blessed.

Beloved, I wish above all things that thou mayest prosper and be in health, even as thy soul prospereth.   —III John 2

THE DIVINE CANNOT LACK FOR ANYTHING, AND WE SHOULD NOT LACK FOR ANYTHING THAT MAKES LIFE WORTH WHILE HERE ON EARTH.
   —*The Science of Mind,* page 262

OUR ENDLESS SUPPLY

I ONCE HEARD a student of metaphysics say that he didn't feel he should do prayer work every day; he only prayed when he felt he really needed help. I guess he figured praying often would use up his quota of good if he wasn't careful! Some people may feel that way, but could it really be possible to pray too much or fear exhausting the resources of the Universe? Could God decide to say, "Okay, enough! You've had your share!"?

God, like a great ocean, constantly rolls waves of good upon the shoreline of our lives. The waters of supply roll on without surcease. Only a consciousness of limitation may cause us to take a thimbleful of good, when we could fill an entire swimming pool! If the nature of God is to withhold no good thing, to willingly fulfill the desire of every heart, where does Divine Supply end except in our belief that there is not enough good to go around? Let us accept everything necessary for a good life, always remembering to give thanks for what we receive.

God is the Sublime Essence of Life, and because I am One with God, Life in Its fullness is mine. I do not hesitate to accept from Divine Abundance everything I need to live well. So long as I take from no one else, I know there is plenty for me. I do not limit my good, since my expectations are high, and I am grateful for every wonderful person, place, and thing that enters my life.

Every good gift and every perfect gift is from above, and cometh down from the Father of lights. . . . —James 1:17

WE ARE TO BE FED, CLOTHED, AND SUPPLIED IN EVERY NEED, STRAIGHT FROM THE CENTER AND SOURCE OF ALL.

—*The Science of Mind,* page 496

OUR LIVELIHOOD

THE WORD "livelihood" is a good way to describe our employment, for our work should be alive and vital to us. If it is not, we are probably in the wrong line of business. Not only that, but our work should also be more than just a way of making money. It should be a means of expressing ourselves in a way that will bring us pride because of what we have accomplished.

To every job which is ours to do, we need to bring at least two things—pride and desire. Pride in our good services rendered and the desire to do our best. When these two qualities are present, no work will keep from us its own hidden treasure (though that treasure may not be apparent to everyone).

Our only employer, ultimately, is God. If God is all substance, and the Source of all that comes to us, then He is the "boss," and what an inspiring ideal it would be for us to do our best work for our spiritual Father, thus transcending all human personality. The "sting" thus disappears from dealing with those who tend to irascibility. And there is always the bonus of unexpected good when one works consciously for God!

There is only one life, God's Life, and I am one with It. **I am in my right place of employment; I like my work; and I bless all the opportunities for growth that it brings me.**

I know that in all my endeavors I do God's work—a blessed, important contribution to life—and I give thanks for the outlet for my talents which my livelihood affords me.

Commit thy works unto the Lord, and thy thoughts shall be established.
—Proverbs 16:3

I SERVE THE WORLD. I WAIT UPON THE LORD WITHIN ALL MEN. . . .
—*The Science of Mind,* page 521

TRUE RICHES

IN MANY OF us there can often be found a small, vague voice which says, "If I had more money, how much easier life would be!" But it isn't necessarily so! In the first place, our thinking is often only wishful and not expectant. We do not believe we were "meant" to have much money. Also, money is not always what we want, but the things that money buys . . . the comforts and luxuries of life.

Going a bit further, we find that we tend to equate the comforts and luxuries of life with contentment. In this regard we have reached a wrong conclusion and should reexamine the basis from which we operate; we may find ourselves working in reverse.

The rich contentment we seek can only be found within ourselves and not in outer things. Because all substance and serenity come from a giving God, we are meant to have money; we are meant to be contented. But our contentment must be born of a balanced inner self, which attracts to us everything we need, including sufficient money for a good life.

There is only one life, God's Life, and I am one with It. **Because I live the Divine Life, I am rich in outer substance and in inner security. All the things that make life joyous and satisfying are mine—good health, abundant resources, productive self-expression, and good friends.**

I gratefully give thanks and cherish my good. I give of my good to others, thus making room for me to receive more blessings and more spiritual growth.

. . . nor trust in uncertain riches, but in the living God, who giveth us richly all things to enjoy. . . . —I Timothy 6:17

LIFE LIES OPEN TO ME—RICH, FULL, ABUNDANT.
—*The Science of Mind*, page 305

THE CREATION OF GOOD BUSINESS PRINCIPLES

THESE DAYS it is very important to get back to the *spirit* of good business and turn away from the disrupting effects we may sometimes encounter among those whose integrity seems questionable. We are basically our own leaders, our own best examples. Outwardly we may seem to work for an individual or institution, but actually we work for the Universe. It can only put forth Its best, for Divine Substance is only of the highest order. So if we are to *receive* the best, according to God's Law we must act in accordance with the highest work ethic we know, one of joy, enthusiasm, and the desire to render a truly useful service.

To work carelessly, indifferently, with the thought only of our own monetary gain, perhaps even undoing the good of another, will ultimately cost us dearly. We may lose a fine position, or worse, our own spiritual integrity may be damaged by the nagging knowledge that we have willingly cheated on ourselves! No fineries can derive from a shattered self-image. We are children of the Most High. We owe It our best efforts.

There is only one life, God's Life, and I am one with It. **Today I rededicate myself to my work and to serving the highest ideal I know—that of the Universal Presence which employs me. To It alone I am ultimately answerable.**

Therefore I set into motion good, constructive causes which benefit all, and I accept good results, both in financial success and in a deeply satisfying job, well done. I am grateful to God for good constantly received.

But let every man prove his own work, and then shall he have rejoicing in himself alone, and not in another. —Galatians 6:4

EVERY MAN MUST PAY THE PRICE FOR THAT WHICH HE RECEIVES AND THAT PRICE IS PAID IN MENTAL AND SPIRITUAL COIN.

—*The Science of Mind*, page 268

HAVE YOU A GOOD MONEY CONSCIOUSNESS?

MANY PEOPLE have mixed feelings about praying for money. Some have such a poor opinion of their abilities that they cannot imagine earning what they need or desire. Others may cling to the old idea that money is somehow "evil" or at least unspiritual. Since money has come to represent the essence of materiality, the spiritually minded may consider it improper to want more.

If, however, we will remember that all matter is simply Spirit compressed into form, we will find that money is Divine Substance with a tangible use for us. Since our universe is based on a spiritual pattern of goodness, no material manifestation of it can be in any way evil.

Let us, then, consider money properly . . . as a product of Spirit, manifesting as good in our lives. Money is a value received for services rendered, and when we earn money or otherwise deserve it, nothing can prevent its freely flowing into our experience. Then when we exchange that money for the goods and services we desire, its circulation will have begun again and the flow will continue—just like all else in God's Universe!

I honor the Divine Presence as the Provider for all creation. All money and the good things of life come from God's storehouse of Abundance, given freely to me in proportion to my ability to accept. Money circulating through my life is a great benefit to all whom it reaches. I bless it, respect its proper value, and give thanks, knowing that what I send forth must return to me multiplied.

Beloved, I wish above all things that thou mayest prosper and be in health, even as thy soul prospereth. —III John 2

I CAN NEVER BE EXHAUSTED, MY GOOD CAN NEVER BE DEPLETED, BECAUSE THAT SOURCE FROM WHICH MY GOOD COMES IS INEXHAUST-IBLE. —*The Science of Mind,* page 293

MY BUSINESS IS PROSPEROUS

THOUGHTS OF recessions, slowdowns, business reversals, "crunches and squeezes," or the Wall Street bulls and bears, can all be fearsome on the surface. Plummeting graphs can cause us to lose confidence in ourselves and in the naturally abundant way of the Universe.

In the face of gloomy predictions, when we are spiritually inclined business people, we remember to turn from the human opinion, no matter how expert it may be, and align ourselves with the Divine Presence. We know that, in an ever-changing Universe, new ideas are coming into being, as are new circumstances which bring opportunities in their wake, and a constant exchange of goods and services which bring benefit and profit to all who are alert to them.

Therefore as business people attuned to such a Presence, we are able to surmount the trends of the times and incline our talents to profitable methods, as we utilize infinite Intelligence.

I accept the abundance and fullness of the inner life that is mine. I know it constantly alerts me to useful new ideas which benefit my business life. I am prosperous and successful because, as God's creation, I do not seek to manifest anything contrary to the nature of God. I am undismayed by human lack of confidence, being assured that I am always in the forefront of prosperous business enterprises. Thank You, God, for this realization!

O Lord, how great are thy works! and thy thoughts are very deep.
—Psalm 92:5

MY AFFAIRS ARE MANAGED BY LOVE, AND DIRECTED BY WISDOM, AND THEY CANNOT FAIL TO PROSPER AND EXPAND.
—*The Science of Mind,* page 523

MONEY CONSCIOUSNESS

HOW PEOPLE habitually use money is almost as important as the amount they have to deal with. Many people pray for more money because they think they probably ought to have more, but they have no specific purpose for the money. Therefore, the image given to Divine Mind to work on is somewhat hazy, and that may delay the arrival of more money. Or . . . people think only of acquiring enough cash to get out of debt, when perhaps their real concern should be learning how to use the money they have, or will have, in a wise manner. They forget that it is just as easy to be in debt while handling a lot of money as it is while handling a little!

If people want to acquire money, they need to develop a good "money-consciousness." And they should make an inner agreement with themselves to take on the responsibility which goes with the extra cash they will be receiving. If they suddenly find themselves with more to spend, it will not endure on the physical level if they do not learn how to put that extra money to its best use. When people decide they need additional cash, they should be willing to channel the money-activity in a wise and thoughtful manner.

The Universal Life and I are one, one in spiritual inspiration, one in matured thought, one in physical action. I know how to handle money with good grace, when to keep it moving, and when to save it. I bless the money as it comes to me and as it goes forth from me, and I return a portion of my money to my spiritual Source, to act as a seed for future returns.

And he shall be like a tree planted by the rivers of water, that bringeth forth his fruit in his season; his leaf also shall not wither; and whatsoever he doeth shall prosper. —Psalm 1:3

THERE IS A CONTINUOUS MOVEMENT TOWARD ME OF SUPPLY, OF MONEY, OF ALL THAT I NEED TO EXPRESS THE FULLEST LIFE, HAPPINESS AND ACTION. —*The Science of Mind*, page 263

PROSPERITY BEGINS AS A FEELING

WHY IS IT that some people make a good salary and yet never seem to have enough money? They continually talk about inflation and keep telling everybody who will listen that they never get a large enough raise to "keep up." Other people may make less money, but always seem to have enough to do nearly everything they want to do. It makes us think that perhaps the amount of money one makes is not nearly so important as how one values and appreciates the money and its use.

By having a *feeling* of prosperity, people can incorporate into their lives the *actuality* of prosperity. For example, some years ago I watched two couples start out with small salaries. Couple No. 1 made more money but had some extra bills to pay, which they resented. They felt squeezed financially. Couple No. 2 had less money but felt there would "always be enough." Couple No. 1 now have a good, predictable salary . . . but still feel the money squeeze. Couple No. 2, living in a costlier house, with one child more and having sustained some temporary interruptions in salary, always have enough money. What can be the difference but the *expectations of prosperity?*

The Universal Life and I are one, one in spiritual inspiration, one in matured thought, one in physical action. The Law of Life prospers me according to my own thoughts about money and I am grateful for the money that comes to me. Not only do I live comfortably, but my money produces a good feeling in me and becomes a wisely used asset.

Wealth and riches shall be in his house: and his righteousness endureth for ever. —Psalm 112:3

IF ONE WISHES TO DEMONSTRATE PROSPERITY, HE MUST FIRST HAVE A CONSCIOUSNESS OF PROSPERITY. . . . —*The Science of Mind*, page 143

LIFE HOLDS GREAT ABUNDANCE

W E LIVE IN an abundant universe . . . there is no getting away from that fact. And we can have a lot of whatever-it-is-we-want when we set the Law in motion, for the Law cannot restrict us from anything we have coming. However, our abundances might not come in a positive form. We can have an abundance of poverty, an abundance of misery, an abundance of limitation, rather than money or happiness or freedom. It all depends upon what we set in motion through Law.

We are sovereign beings living on a planet which is intended for our good. God has let us alone to use His gifts as we choose, and if we make ignorant choices, we can create a shambles out of what should be Eden.

It is time to learn to work with Law and Its process of right return. Limited mental constructions can only bring an abundance of lack, an abundance of pain or misery. But, right living, right thinking, and right loving bring abundant returns of money, happiness, and serenity.

God is perfect Life, and this Life moves through me progressively as inspiration, thought, and action. Through intuitive wisdom and well-considered thought, I work in accord with the Law of Mind. I do not fear It, for It is the friend which responds to my thoughts. My thoughts are wise, positive. Thus Law returns to me positive, fruitful, physical results. I am attuned to the right action of life within me, and I am thankful.

Be not deceived; God is not mocked: for whatsoever a man soweth, that shall he also reap. —Galatians 6:7

FREE YOURSELF FOREVER FROM THE THOUGHT THAT GOD MAY BE PLEASED BY A LIFE OF SACRIFICE, THAT THE WORLD IS ANY BETTER BECAUSE OF YOUR MISERY, OR THAT RIGHTEOUSNESS IS MORE PERFECTLY EXPRESSED THROUGH POVERTY THAN ABUNDANCE.

—*The Science of Mind,* page 288

MONEY

IF THERE is a lack of money in our lives, we should make sure we harbor no guilty feelings about the desire for money. There is nothing unspiritual about needing or wanting more money, for money is only a means of bringing to us a portion of the universal abundance that is proffered to all. In itself, money is neither good nor bad. It is a medium of exchange that man has devised. In fact, money needs *us* to have any value at all!

If we know that God's good is always available to us and it may come in the form of money, can money be denied us? The answer must be no, for otherwise, it would imply a God which both gives and takes away. Our belief is in a God who only gives!

But any belief in lack or in our own unworthiness can keep money from us. It is important, therefore, for us to know we are creations of the Almighty, creatures of infinite worth. We have the right to as much money as our consciousness can accept, remembering always that what is done to us, is done according to our faith.

I turn now to the Source of every good, and accept my abundance as it comes to me in the form of money. I know that I have a right to earn and enjoy money. God gives to me in proportion to my ability to accept, and my acceptance is now enlarged. I realize my own worth, and my efficient and productive acts verify this evaluation. I am grateful for my money, and seek to use it unselfishly by passing on a portion of it to others. Being faithful in this, I know the channel of my abundance is always open.

A faithful man shall abound with blessings. . . .   —Proverbs 28:20

IF ONE WILL HAVE FAITH IN HIMSELF, FAITH IN HIS FELLOWMEN, IN THE UNIVERSE, AND IN GOD, THAT FAITH WILL LIGHT THE PLACE IN WHICH HE FINDS HIMSELF, AND BY THE LIGHT OF THIS FAITH, HE WILL BE ABLE TO SEE THAT ALL IS GOOD.   —*The Science of Mind,* page 158

AREN'T WE RICH NOW?

T HERE IS A charming story of a newly married young
couple gazing fondly at some lovely furnishings
displayed in a department store window. The young bride
sighs wistfully and says, "Someday we'll be rich." But the
young husband, smiling at his bride, says, "Dear one, we *are*
rich . . . and someday we'll have money!"

No one can listen to that story without a knowing smile.
We *are* rich, aren't we? We are God-gifted with a talent for
living, with our own unique individuality. We have been put
on this earth to discover our Divinity and to utilize Its power
in our lives. An inner Presence is ever nudging us, awaiting
our allowing It to guide us. We can never remain lost,
defeated, or alone unless we wish to, for the Divine Presence
is always ready to lavish Itself on us.

**God *is all Supply,* and living in God's Presence I accept the
material abundance I need.**

The riches of His universe are within my being.

**In and through me are manifested the attributes of God,
for I, as God's creation, must contain the same rich substance
as the Creator.**

**I live a life of affluence based on Divinely given values,
and I accept with thanks these treasures today!**

---

*The blessing of the Lord, it maketh rich, and he addeth no sorrow with
it.* —Proverbs 10:22

. . . BELIEVING THAT THERE IS AN INFINITE LAW OF THE SPIRIT, OR LAW
OF LIFE, WHICH TENDS TO MULTIPLY OUR GIFTS . . . WE MAY ASSUME
THAT SPIRITUAL MAN IS ALREADY A SUCCESS, IS ALREADY SUPPLIED WITH
EVERYTHING THAT HE NEEDS. —*The Science of Mind,* page 270

I AM A FINANCIAL SUCCESS

WE KNOW THAT a certain amount of money is necessary for a comfortable life—and we are entitled to a comfortable life. God does not think more of us if we are poor and in want. In fact, the Universe lies in wait to give us Its abundance. It would shower every blessing upon us if we were but in a proper mental circumstance to receive.

If we are experiencing lack in a Universe of abundance, it can only mean we are at cross-purposes with the innate Goodness of Life. Let us resolve, then, to align our thoughts with ideas of prosperity. Let us cease to limit the areas from which money can come to us. Money, like all form and physical substance, has a spiritual basis, and basically therefore, it must be good.

Money is ours to have, as much as we can accept and circulate. In our exercise of prosperity, let us remember also that a portion of our money should be returned to our spiritual source . . . a seed, as it were, planted for renewed crops of financial success.

Money needs me for proper use and enlarged circulation. I desire money and accept it for my good purposes. I bless my money, knowing it is a form of God's substance, meant for my good. I give thanks as it comes to me and I bless it as it goes forth from me, that all who receive it may also prosper. I give thanks for a constant outflow from God's storehouse of Abundance. Mine is a prosperous life.

For unto every one that hath shall be given, and he shall have abundance: but from him that hath not shall be taken away even that which he hath. —Matthew 25:29

FREE YOURSELF FOREVER FROM THE THOUGHT THAT GOD MAY BE PLEASED BY A LIFE OF SACRIFICE . . . OR THAT RIGHTEOUSNESS IS MORE PERFECTLY EXPRESSED THROUGH POVERTY THAN ABUNDANCE.
—*The Science of Mind,* page 288

WE WORK FOR GOD

ALL OF US who are working people will have times when we wonder whether we are really making any progress on the job. These can be depressing moments, since we invest so much of ourselves and our time in the work we do.

But, all unpleasantness and drudgery can be eliminated on these occasions when we remember that we are really working for God. God is the Source of all substance and supply, and with such an Employer we cannot help but make progress. When we realize this, we also may get added "fringe benefits" we had not expected, in the way of better relations with our supervisors and colleagues.

When we eliminate the idea of "What am I going to get out of this?" and substitute "How much good can I give?" . . . we may be surprised at the happy "getting" our giving will stimulate. Universal Law cannot refuse to work. It will always supply us with the equivalent of what we give, whether what we give is intelligent effort or lackluster effort, flexible attitudes or stilted opinions.

I am happy, prosperous, and fulfilled in my work, as I joyously perform my duties for God. My services and talents are needed; they are expanded by right attitudes and good efforts.

I know I am always in my right place, and this place increases in meaning as my consciousness of good expands. My money comes directly from God. My security comes from God. Therefore, I work freely and fearlessly.

I bless my work and am blessed in it.

. . . every good tree bringeth forth good fruit. . . . —Matthew 7:17

AS WE BRING OURSELVES TO A GREATER VISION, WE INDUCE A GREATER CONCEPT AND THEREBY DEMONSTRATE MORE IN OUR EXPERIENCE.
—*The Science of Mind,* page 282

THE SUBSTANCE OF SPIRIT

WHEN WE are in business and desire a greater flow of goods and services, we are taught to pray believing that our needed increase comes about through the auspices of Spirit. But how is this apparent gap between the spiritual and the material bridged? How can an invisible Presence bring us concrete material things?

Let us remember that the material world is one of *forms*, and that these forms are filled with Spirit. Some of the forms are God-created, while others are created by God's working through mankind. When the forms are man-created, they may be accidental and unintentional, or they may be ones we create deliberately through prayer work.

If, then, there is an apparent lack in our business affairs, Spirit will rush in to fill that lack as soon as we make a specific affirmation, creating a form for it to fill. That is one of God's ways of providing us with everything we need for a good life. We give thanks for the good that is ours and by an enlightened awareness, use this good beneficially for ourselves and for those whom we contact, thus increasing our capacity for receiving even greater good.

God, the only Life there is, and I are joyously one. I affirm that Spirit becomes substance in my world of affairs. I know that no good thing is lacking, for it is the desire of Spirit to fulfill my every need. I accept my increased good business gratefully. Through Divine guidance, I wisely use this substance for the enhancement of myself and all who participate in my activities.

It is the spirit that quickeneth; the flesh profiteth nothing. . . .
—John 6:63

IT IS ALL THE SAME—ONE SUBSTANCE IN THE UNIVERSE, TAKING DIFFERENT FORMS AND SHAPES AND BECOMING DIFFERENT THINGS.
—*The Science of Mind,* page 116

ENJOY YOUR PROSPERITY

A MONG GOD'S blessings to us is our ability to make money, and to exchange it for the good things of life. Money has the power to be converted into the necessities and luxuries we need and want. Why shouldn't we desire it? Why shouldn't we have the amounts of money our consciousness can encompass?

This material world has many lessons to teach us, and among them is a proper regard for what money is and what it does. We are not made more worthy by suffering through lack, nor are we necessarily elevated over others if we have acquired wealth.

There is no logic in our believing that God would present this wonderful planet to us and then expect us to be miserable because we can't get enough. There *is* enough on this abundant earth to sustain life richly. Our task is to respect, to use, and to share God's gift of the earth and its resources, knowing there is plenty of everything for all.

Divine Wisdom indwells me and guides me to the means of experiencing the good things in life that I desire. Today I become more expert at living a balanced life by respecting God's Earth and using its blessings of prosperity wisely. My good is here and I accept it gratefully. I stand, with outstretched arms, to receive this bounty.

. . . the manifestation of the Spirit is given to every man to profit withal.
—I Corinthians 12:7

ANYTHING THAT WILL ENABLE US TO EXPRESS GREATER LIFE, GREATER HAPPINESS, GREATER POWER—SO LONG AS IT DOES NOT HARM ANYONE—MUST BE THE WILL OF GOD FOR US.   —*The Science of Mind*, page 269

V

To Your Other Joys

"**M**AN DOES NOT live by bread alone," and neither do his inner senses. When all the immediate requirements of his mind and body seem cared for, man's more subtle needs then demand attention. As Walt Whitman said, "You are not all included between your hat and your boots." It is perhaps this finer sense which makes you truly what you are, what you were meant to be.

Many people feel these stirrings within themselves but have little direction about what to do to satisfy their inner selves. Thus, I am entrusting to you the following commentaries, which are designed to broaden the vistas of your mind and help you realize more than ever the wonderful person you truly are. You are more than a producer of goods. You are more than a member of a family or an organization. You are more than the total of all the roles you play in life. You are a member of a Cosmic Order which is individualized in you, and you are bound by an inner urging to fulfill an infinite potential. Read these pages with a feeling of celebration at the wonders of you!

Here's to your Other Joys!

TAKE IT EASY

H AVE YOU ever been so rushed that you picked up an object only to drop it right away? Of course you have. We have all snatched things up thinking we had a firm hold on them, only to have them slip right through our fingers. A good guess as to the reason would be that we were in too great a hurry.

Many times we will find that spiritual advancement has also slipped through our fingers because we moved ahead too swiftly, with too tenuous a hold on what we thought we knew. Racing ahead with our presumed accomplishment, we discover that the insight we had, or the concept we suddenly understood, was not the equivalent of our having embodied a consciousness of that thing. Had the lure of "instant understanding" been too great? Did we think that "reading books and saying words" would bring miracles?

Let's consider taking it easy, then. As long as we are sincere in our seeking to be one with God, there's no need to hurry, for the universe is already unfolding at exactly the proper speed.

God gives me complete understanding, and with a deep, unhurried sense of joy I look to the inner Wisdom for revelation. Slowly, serenely, I walk the pathway of discovery through meditation and I study upon it.

My faith and understanding are firm and well-grounded as I scale the heights of spiritual consciousness, assured of the complete realization of my God-nature.

For this deeper perception of infinite Wisdom, I give thanks.

. . . Behold, I lay in Zion for a foundation a stone, a tried stone, a precious corner stone, a sure foundation: he that believeth shall not make haste. —Isaiah 28:16

. . . LIFE WAITS UPON MAN'S DISCOVERY OF NATURAL LAWS, HIS DISCOVERY OF HIMSELF, AND HIS DISCOVERY OF HIS RELATIONSHIP TO THE GREAT WHOLE. —*The Science of Mind*, page 72

HOW TO OVERCOME DISAPPOINTMENT

I T WOULD BE impossible for us to avoid disappointments. Things simply will not always go as we would have them, nor will people always respond to us as we would desire. But disappointment *can* lose its "sting" once we understand what it may actually represent.

One reason for disappointment, for instance, is often that we seek to maneuver people or circumstances in certain directions of our own choosing. However if we have done this after first allowing God to "make straight the way" . . . after declaring that what we really seek is the highest good of all concerned . . . then if things do not evolve as we feel they should, we may be sure that, with God in charge, something better and more appropriate is coming along. The disappointment, therefore, is temporary and basically insignificant.

In trusting God to align us with what is the highest and best for us, we may not always immediately recognize the God-ordained developments, but we may be certain they are there.

God's Life is my life, and I place all my endeavors under His guidance. I let Divine Wisdom direct all my plans, thus insuring the best possible outcomes for everyone involved. I take disappointments in my stride, for elements unknown to me are not unknown to God. Divine right action is always at work in my activities, and I gratefully accept its harvest of good.

Search me, O God, and know my heart: try me, and know my thoughts. . . . —Psalm 139:23

STAY WITH THE ONE AND NEVER DEVIATE FROM IT, NEVER LEAVE IT FOR A MOMENT. —*The Science of Mind*, page 282

DO WE LEARN FROM OUR SETBACKS?

E RNEST HOLMES stated that "the world has learned all it should through suffering." Suffering is not God-ordained. But, being human and often inclined to making self-limiting choices, we create setbacks for ourselves. Setbacks do have educational value. Do we gain from them, though? Or do we resent the spot in which we find ourselves?

Someone has suggested that "man's extremity is God's opportunity." Let's face it! The unfortunate fact is that we sometimes have to end up flat on our backs before we will give God the go-ahead in our lives!

If a person has need for a doctor's care or for hospitalization, he may tend to feel guilty or resentful about the mental misstep he is certain caused his problem. Instead, he should be utilizing the time for blessed rest or reflection. He should recognize the need for an overdue mental vacation and really "rest in the Lord." Let us bless these aids which alleviate our pains, even while we endeavor to rise above the need to suffer!

God is my wholeness, and I am immersed in an awareness of God. I am thankful for the understanding that enables me to learn from adversity.

When temporary setbacks appear, I look confidently to the Divine for quiet sustenance, solution, and refreshing ideas, knowing that my patience results in a clear, unobstructed answer.

God *sees me as perfect.* I trust in His expression of Wholeness through me, this moment.

Rest in the Lord, and wait patiently for him. . . .   —Psalm 37:7

GOD NEVER INTENDED MAN TO SUFFER. SUFFERING MAY BE SALUTARY IN THAT IT LEADS US TO A PLACE WHERE WE LEARN THAT IT IS UNNECESSARY!   —*The Science of Mind,* page 109

NEW THOUGHTS FOR OLD

L ET'S LOOK for a moment at a scene from one of childhood's favorite stories, *Aladdin or the Wonderful Lamp.* We will remember that a greedy official enticed the magic lamp away from Aladdin's household with the inviting offer of "new lamps for old." The lamp was not his for long, though, because it never really belonged to him in the first place.

Isn't "new life for old" our desire? We wish to supplant old and perhaps painful ways of living with newer, happier ones, and this requires the inlay of new thought-patterns. But if we, like the greedy official, merely wish for something that isn't yet ours and make a hasty grab for it, we either may not keep it long or it will give us little pleasure. It will not really belong to us.

If we are to exchange "new life for old," we first must fully embody the appropriate states of mind. Then we will be able to acquire and keep the good things of life, for they will be a part of our whole consciousness.

God *is my constant Renewer.* In His nature I live and move and have my being. I resolve now to lift my consciousness to a keener awareness of the reality of good that God has for me.

I monitor my thinking, and sustain only the mental and spiritual equivalent of the things I desire, loosing all ideas of unworthiness.

God ever holds out His fullness of Life, which I now accept, and I gratefully give thanks for my increased supply of every good.

———————

For if there be first a willing mind, it is accepted according to that a man hath, and not according to that he hath not. —II Corinthians 8:12

THE LAW IS INFINITE AND PERFECT BUT IN ORDER TO MAKE A DEMONSTRATION WE MUST HAVE A MENTAL EQUIVALENT OF THE THING WE DESIRE. —*The Science of Mind,* page 281

RIGHT EFFORT

IF WE WORK in conjunction with Infinite Intelligence, we can expect to achieve without strain. But let's not confuse strain with effort, for very little is ever accomplished without effort. This title of a book by Lao Russell gives a very perceptive example: *God Will Work With You But Not For You.*

Teaming up with the Infinite is a two-way affair! God may provide the idea, the know-how, and the means, but we must provide the "zip" that makes realities of intentions. Not every aspect of work can be entertaining or fun. Parts of it will require ordinary hard effort, which in itself can be a great lesson in patience and perseverance.

Is it "manna from heaven" that we want . . . with all our desires magically manifesting before us effortlessly? Isn't it true that things easily gained are often lightly valued? The child soon tires of toys that are constantly given by indulgent parents or grandparents. Great effort, however, constructively directed, can bring deep soul satisfaction . . . and all the while God is working *with* you!

God, my infinite Partner, is inspiring me all the way, so I am not discouraged or hesitant about putting forth my best work to achieve worthy goals. No energy is wasted, for I know there are great lessons to be learned in well-directed effort. Though I work diligently, I work serenely. I am confident of an Infinite Guidance, and I gratefully accept the joy of attaining my occupational goal through energetic cooperation with God. In this consciousness of faith and work, I know fulfillment.

For as the body without the spirit is dead, so faith without works is dead also. —James 2:26

EVERY MAN MUST PAY THE PRICE FOR THAT WHICH HE RECEIVES AND THAT PRICE IS PAID IN MENTAL AND SPIRITUAL COIN.
—*The Science of Mind*, page 268

A HOLY CURIOSITY

DON'T WE ALL know people whom time appears to have bypassed? We may see them regularly for years, and somehow they don't seem to be getting any older.

Although they are surely taking good care of their bodies, it is probably a safe bet to say they are also possessed by what Einstein termed a "holy curiosity." Without curiosity, mental circulation may stop and the problems of age can begin. But when curiosity is active, mental circulation continues. The curious person is naturally open to new ideas and is always sifting through thoughts, rejecting those which inhibit life and absorbing those which enhance life.

Curiosity is one of the greatest mental preservatives that a person can have. It is cultivated by the mind hungry to know all the wonders of life. Let us remain open, then, to Spirit's influx of ideas and keep our curiosity alive so time adds life to our years rather than years to our life.

God is perfect Life, and this Life moves through me progressively as inspiration, thought, and action. I am an open channel through which Divine ideas flow endlessly. My mind is active and ever young, responsive and resilient, unheeding of the static confines defined as age. Life in all its goodness is, indeed, holy to me; and I treasure every opportunity to express more of its gifts. I am grateful for the easy movement of ideas within me.

Give ye ear, and hear my voice; hearken, and hear my speech.
—Isaiah 28:23

MAN IS BIRTHLESS, DEATHLESS, AGELESS SPIRIT; AND THIS SHOULD BE THE CONSCIOUSNESS OF OUR WORK.
—*The Science of Mind,* page 239

THE EXERCISE OF JOY

JOY IS A very singular emotion. For one thing, it can never become commonplace in our lives, while other emotions may. We can come to take our successes, our satisfactions, even our loves, for granted. However, when we are joyous, we find we cannot be complacent *at the same time.* Whenever we feel joy, it is as if something within us were vigorously trying to escape the boundaries of our bodies. We feel elated, uplifted, lighter than air. When we are joyous, we are touched by God's wonderful activity within us.

The opinion of that great metaphysical writer Thomas Troward was that God's enjoyment is to see Himself in expression through man. In fact, Troward felt that Spirit's enjoyment of Life was limitless. Consequently, as Divine recipients of God's "joie de vivre," our capacity for joy must be limitless also! Are we engaging in the "exercise of joy" every day? Does it fill us with wonder, freshen our outlook, and expand our minds and bodies with the deep, wholesome breath of Spirit? Today let's allow joy to increase in us tenfold, one hundredfold, one thousandfold!

God is perfect Life, and this Life moves through me progressively as inspiration, thought, and action. I am alive to the quality of joy in me today. Everything I perceive is pleasing and everyone responds to me favorably. I cannot help but be enthusiastic about my life and my loves, for Divine joy in me bubbles into happy laughter and harmonious experiences. I give thanks for my joyful nature.

Then will I go unto the altar of God, unto God my exceeding joy. . . .
—Psalm 43:4

IF WE GAZE LONGINGLY AT JOY, IT WILL MAKE ITS HOME WITH US, AND WE SHALL ENTER ITS PORTALS AND BE HAPPY.
—*The Science of Mind,* page 491

GOD IS UNEXPECTED GOOD

ONE DELIGHTFUL consequence of spiritual growth is receiving unexpected good . . . when our inner progress takes outer form as a surprising and happy manifestation.

Since our life sustenance comes from limitless Spirit, and since we continually make gains in consciousness through study and practice of what we have learned, this sustenance becomes progressively greater. Through accumulations of spiritual awareness . . . which often come so subtly we don't realize they are upon us . . . we become heir to the "nifties" that a more elevated level of living brings to us. And one day, suddenly, there is some unlooked-for good at our doorstep!

Many times we think of unforeseen good as some material thing, but it can come in many forms. If, for instance, we give a gift of service to Life out of love, without any strings attached, Life will repay the gift with a wonderful piece of unexpected good . . . perhaps a loving friend, perhaps a delightful new set of circumstances. We should simply go along our spiritual way, always alert and ready to enjoy any unexpected good as it comes to us.

The Universal Life and I are one, one in spiritual inspiration, one in matured thought, one in physical action. I know that I live completely with the life of God and I am therefore surrounded by good.

As I become more aware of God-qualities, I am open to good around me which hitherto went unrecognized. I give of myself lovingly and willingly, knowing that from God's great storehouse of good, I am ever replenished.

Blessed are they which do hunger and thirst after righteousness: for they shall be filled. —Matthew 5:6

AS MUCH LIFE AS ONE CAN CONCEIVE WILL BECOME A PART OF HIS EX-PERIENCE. —*The Science of Mind,* page 269

THE ART OF GHOST CHASING

G HOST STORIES were a favorite pastime for many of us as children . . . wrathful creatures that haunted houses tantalized and mystified us. Perhaps some of us are still terrified of "ghosts-of-the-unknown," or we are frightened by phantom ideas in our own minds which haunt our activities and inhibit our growth. How many of us still have "skeletons" in our mental closets, the rattling bones of fear, resentment, hatred, or bigotry? If these limiting ideas remained in the background, they would be bad enough, but they eventually take on distinct shapes in our lives . . . such as those of sickness, business failure, and friendlessness. Therefore we cannot allow such mental apparitions to remain with us.

The bright beams of inspired, spiritual daylight can chase away the ghosts of limitation from our experiences. So we owe it to ourselves to exorcise unhappy thought patterns and replace them with the solid spirit of Love. Then we need never fear things that go bump in the nighttime of mental or spiritual ignorance.

The Universal Life and I are one, one in spiritual inspiration, one in matured thought, one in physical action. I believe in the innate goodness of life, and that the Universe brings only beneficial experiences to me as I release myself from the cloudy thoughts of limitation. No longer am I haunted by the ghosts of past mistakes, for I am free from any power they once had over me. I give thanks to a wonderful Creator, who gives me numberless opportunities to take advantage of Divine goodness.

. . . for the Lord searcheth all hearts, and understandeth all the imaginations of the thoughts. . . . —I Chronicles 28:9

THOUGHTS OF LACK, POVERTY, AND LIMITATION CONTAIN WITHIN THEMSELVES THE CONDITIONS NECESSARY TO PRODUCE LACK, POVERTY AND LIMITATION. —*The Science of Mind*, page 402

A TIGER BY THE TAIL

PEOPLE WHO enter into mental and spiritual study will soon find that they are holding a glorious tiger by the tail! Because once we advance spiritually even a little bit—we simply cannot let go. When that door to the greater powers of the mind is opened, wonderful qualities of life pour through it . . . qualities for which we then become responsible . . . qualities that we must take charge of.

An awakened spiritual mentality leaves us forever changed; we are no longer content to slog along through life as we once did. Suddenly we may even feel protective about our awakening consciousness, as we are driven to experience more and more of the wonderful Presence we have allowed to enter our lives. We become more sensitive to everything— so we may also find it necessary to be on guard against possible erosion of consciousness. Mostly, the awakening is a happy concern; however, it is well worthwhile to spend time reinforcing this new consciousness by prayer and meditation, so nothing dims the golden light of increased understanding.

The Universal Life and I are one, one in spiritual inspiration, one in matured thought, one in physical action. I am fearless in my pursuit of spiritual understanding, and I accept the responsibility for care of my blossoming awareness. This wonderful feeling of increasing revelation of my oneness with God is worth all the time and effort I have to give. I am secure from harmful outer influences and I go forth joyously along the path of unfoldment.

. . .put on the new man, which is renewed in knowledge after the image of him that created him. . . . —Colossians 3:10

THE DIVINE URGE WITHIN US IS GOD'S WAY OF LETTING US KNOW THAT WE SHOULD PUSH FORWARD AND TAKE THAT WHICH IS AWAITING OUR DEMAND. —*The Science of Mind*, page 157

THE PERSONALNESS OF GOD

E RNEST HOLMES spoke many times of the "warmth and color" of God. He felt that the Infinite is "personal to all who believe in Its Presence!" Emmet Fox remarked that God has every quality of personality except its limitation. And the Master himself brought the creative Principle down to earth by constantly calling It the "Father."

To consider God strictly as a lawful, scientific, eternal Process, therefore, would be to take away our ability to feel "close" to our Creator. No one can feel close to a dry, impersonal Process. Besides that, a lack of Divine intimacy would prohibit the development of our sensitive, intuitive nature, that part of us which contains the esthetic qualities of artistry and imagination. God as Love is intensely personal to His creation, for there is no tenderness or compassion in man that cannot be first found in God. Recognizing this personalness of God reassures us that our good comes to us through God's desire to give to us. He responds to us by responding through us, intimately in every heart.

God, infinite Personality, enlivens and enriches me this day with a deep sense of livingness. God is closer to me than my own heartbeat and responds to me as a loving Father. I never feel lonely or rejected, for I am a desired creation, intimately sharing the great heart of God. I am never separated from my good. I gratefully accept a life of greater warmth and fulfillment. And so it is.

The Father loveth the Son, and hath given all things into his hand.
—John 3:35

SPIRITUAL EVOLUTION SHOULD MAKE THE INFINITE NOT MORE DISTANT; BUT MORE INTIMATE. —*The Science of Mind,* page 89

RELEASE UNDUE RESPONSIBILITY

ISN'T IT A relief to know that, unlike the mythological Atlas, we do not have to bear the whole world upon our shoulders? We need not worry about keeping the earth in orbit, the seasons in order, or the growth process in motion. We know that God is perfectly capable of attending to these monumental tasks. We also believe that we have access to this Divine Power which orders the Universe and that we can use It for our own purposes. Why then do we run our private affairs with such difficulty?

Could it be that we forget to "render unto God" the things which are His to do—the outworking of our affairs in an orderly, lawful manner? Are we of such little faith that we take the whole burden of determining how, when, and what kind of a thing shall occur in our lives, forgetting that God, in infinite Wisdom, may have even better things planned?

Of course we know this, but daily busyness often robs us of the constructive awareness that we are always under Divine Care. Therefore, let us allow God's universe to unfold, free from the limitations we might shortsightedly impose.

There is only one life, God's Life, and I am one with It. **I am certain of God's Wisdom and Guidance in all my affairs. Therefore, having done my prayer work, I release my activities to God, trusting Him for just and timely demonstrations.**

I do not tamper with Divine right action, knowing It brings that which is more wonderful than I could imagine! I am deeply thankful.

. . . Render therefore unto Caesar the things which are Caesar's; and unto God the things that are God's. —Matthew 22:21

. . . WE SHOULD BE CAREFUL, AFTER THE TREATMENT HAS BEEN GIVEN, THAT WE TAKE NO RESPONSIBILITY OF TRYING TO MAKE IT WORK.
—*The Science of Mind*, page 318

LIVING WITHOUT FEAR

I AM PRIVILEGED to know a truly fearless gentleman. He is no fool about placing his well-being in deliberate jeopardy, but he lives each day with the expectancy that everything in life is his to have. He does not fear failure, competition, or illness. He knows completely and without reservation where his true Sustenance comes from, and he is wise enough to know that no person can keep him from his good.

Such an attitude sounds almost too good to be true, doesn't it? Perhaps even a little foolhardy. But I assure you it is not. My friend is an unassuming, natural person and is very seldom disappointed in any area of life. He expects the best, and he gets it. He is a student of the Science of Mind who truly practices its precepts.

How difficult would it be for us to unlimber ourselves and start living fearlessly? Do we not believe that God is our endless Good, our constant Friend and Protector? If we so believe, then let us live accordingly . . . a life of freedom, trust, and limitlessness.

God is the Sublime Essence of Life, and because I am One with God, Life in Its fullness is mine. I feel as if a great weight has been lifted from my shoulders, for I now live without fear. I believe that God maintains me in every way, that I lack nothing, and that the best is mine to have. No one and no thing can hinder me, for I am God's beloved and grateful child.

. . . Why are ye so fearful? how is it that ye have no faith?
—Mark 4:40

ALL DOUBT AND FEAR MUST GO AND IN THEIR PLACE MUST COME FAITH AND CONFIDENCE, FOR WE SHALL BE LED BY THE SPIRIT INTO ALL GOOD.
—*The Science of Mind*, page 272

SIMPLICITY

UNDERLYING our every daily act, however complicated it may seem, there is an innate simplicity. All too often, though, this is clouded over by rapid, high-powered living, as the Space Age has fooled us into believing that we must go about everything in a complicated fashion, creating grandiose mountains where molehills would do.

Remember watching a cat curled up alongside a person it loved? Such utter contentment it showed in being near one who was important. Nothing could have been more beautiful than that simple act of devotion, and we can take a lesson from such an animal, remembering likewise to draw near the Divine Spirit which is always closer to us than our own breath. We need not scatter our forces by giving insurmountable power to the tasks that beset us. If we truly believe that God is omnipresent, that God is the only Knower, then our reliance upon Him will be unswerving. Nothing could be simpler than that. Plain, uncomplicated trust in Infinite Intelligence will take the element of stress out of our lives, and we will be a fountain of happy accomplishment.

I *know* that all my needs are met daily by the infinite Knower, who answers before I call. I immerse myself in Spirit. Every obstacle in my path of unfoldment is dissolved, and I view everything in its proper perspective. I give no undue importance to superficialities, keeping my life unbound and uncluttered by drawing ever nearer to God. I know that my real treasures lie deep within me and manifest as I reveal my God-nature.

In all thy ways acknowledge him, and he shall direct thy paths.
—Proverbs 3:6

THERE IS NO OVER-ACTION NOR INACTION IN DIVINE LAW, FOR EVERYTHING MOVES ACCORDING TO PERFECT HARMONY.
—*The Science of Mind,* page 524

GOOD HUMOR

NEVER BEFORE has it been so necessary to possess the uplifting qualities of a light heart and the spontaneity of ready laughter. With the newspapers and television full of tense situations, we can very easily become embroiled in the "heaviness" of living. But laughter has the Godlike touch of being able to take the sting out of difficult circumstances. It acts like salt, enhancing the things that are good and making palatable those things which are less pleasant.

I think of a college professor of mine. She was not considered good-looking, but she transmitted such a sunniness and a charming wit in all her presentations that she was one of the most popular and effective teachers in the whole school.

This winning quality of the Divine nature is to be found in all of us, for God does not give to some and refuse others. We may, however, need to remove the dross of unhappy outlooks and frequent complaining to find our own joy. Why should we approach God so seriously and gravely? Divine Love has a much freer channel through a happy heart than It ever does through a heavy heart!

I *know* that joy is a more accurate projection of my Divine nature than a long face and an attitude of pious martyrdom. The true Self of myself is full of the vibrancy of life, for God's Love could never express in an unhappy manner. I feel this inner Presence now as an upwelling of quiet assurance that is never discouraged or touched by despair. As I present a pleasant outlook, I attract the same wonderful attitude from those around me, for what I put into the Law of Mind with conviction, I must experience in return.

All the days of the afflicted are evil: but he that is of a merry heart hath a continual feast. —Proverbs 15:15

MY SOUL WITHIN ME REJOICES AT THE REALIZATION OF LIFE. I AM MADE GLAD AS I BEHOLD MY INNER LIGHT. . . .
—*The Science of Mind*, page 516

ENTHUSIASM

I REMEMBER A delightful person who was happily addicted to the use of superlatives. Nothing was ever "fine" or "all right." Everything she undertook turned out to be "magnificent." If we adopt this attitude ourselves, we will discover a genuine zest in doing even the simplest things in life. And why should living be otherwise? Each one of us is a product of God's urge to express more of Himself through us. Life imparts to us so much of magnificence, how can we be satisfied in living anything less?

Every rose petal stretches itself out to its fullest as it blooms. Every tree grows to the greatest height it can reach. Every child making mudpies gloriously immerses himself up to his elbows in this happy task. When Jesus said that we should "become as little children," he was referring to this wholehearted, intuitive approach to life. As we grow to enlightened adulthood, this inner urge to express life to its utmost should be heightened. The more we realize our Godlike nature, the more strongly this Divine Force will flow into everything we do.

I *know* that I am an individualization of the Divine, which is ever seeking expression through me. I let nothing stand in Its way. I greet every day with a melody in my heart and a joyous prayer on my lips. Everything I do deserves my fullest attention. Every idea that comes to me shows me another chance for growth, another means to discover more of the truth about myself—that I live and move and have my being in God, and simply must express more, never less, of this God-Life.

Happy is the man that findeth wisdom, and the man that getteth understanding. —Proverbs 3:13

I AM FILLED WITH THE JOY OF THE SPIRIT, AND I OVERFLOW WITH THE GLADNESS OF LIFE. —*The Science of Mind*, page 539

WHEN DAY IS DONE

EVERY DAY is full of challenges, some of them joyous, some of them disturbing; and when night falls, we may still be working mentally with various of our problems. We are wise, however, not to attempt to sleep on a truly upsetting situation, for the subconscious mind, which never sleeps, will tend to pick up that strong disturbance and continue working on it throughout the night. Then the next morning we may awaken still tired and upset, without the refreshment that sleep should have given us.

Let us remember at the end of each day to collect all our concerns and give them over to the Father. Let Him dissipate all disappointments, annoyances, and misdirected emotions. If we need the answer to a question or solution to a problem, we will be much more receptive to that answer from Divine Mind if our own minds are clear of disruption. In God is our well of peace, available night and day. As we release the cares of the day to God, our nights will bring the necessary renewal —as they should.

God, the only Life there is, and I are joyously one. At the end of each day, I release my concerns to God, knowing that Divine Peace neutralizes all worry and doubt. I sleep quietly and serenely, and I awaken with a keen, clear mind. I am open to Divine guidance and receive all I need to know for the conduct of my daily affairs. I give thanks for successful days and peaceful nights.

And let the peace of God rule in your hearts, to the which also ye are called in one body; and be ye thankful. —Colossians 3:15

THROUGH THE LONG NIGHT PEACE REMAINS WITH ME, AND AT THE BREAKING OF THE NEW DAY I SHALL STILL BE FILLED WITH LIFE AND LOVE. —*The Science of Mind,* page 526

If you would like to learn about our other publications or any of the ideas discussed in this book, you are cordially invited to write the publishers. There is no obligation. You may use the card adjacent to this page, or if it has been removed, write:

SCIENCE OF MIND PUBLICATIONS
Dept. SL
P.O. Box 75127
Los Angeles, CA 90075